To

_____

From

_____

Date

_____

ON THE GO
FAMILY
DEVOTION

# JOURNEYING TOGETHER

## *Family Devotional*

## FOR FAMILIES WITH PRESCHOOL AND ELEMENTARY KIDS

### MATT AND NOEL GUEVARA

An imprint of Hendrickson Publishers Marketing, LLC.
Peabody, Massachusetts
www.HendricksonRose.com

On the Go Family Devotion: Journeying Together Devotional For Families with Preschool and Elementary Kids
©2017, Matt and Noel Guevara

RoseKidz®
An imprint of Hendrickson Publishers Marketing, LLC.
P. O. Box 3473, Peabody, MA 01961-3473
www.HendricksonRose.com

Register your book at www. HendricksonRose.com/register and receive a free Bible Reference download.

Cover and interior design by Nancy L. Haskins
Cover photo by Alliance
Animal illustrations by tn-prints

ISBN 10: 1-628625-01-5
ISBN 13: 978-1-628625-01-1
RoseKidz® reorder #L50006
Religion/Christian Life/Devotional

Printed in South Korea

## DEDICATION

To Bel, Sof, Z and Josie: Thanks for filling
our life with so many stories, and for making
this journey an incredible adventure. We love you
deeply. And to the children, we met through Safe
Families, who crossed our path and then continued:
Our journey would be incomplete without you.
We remember you always.

## NICE WORDS ABOUT JOURNEYING

Matt and Noel get that parenting, like discipleship, is an unscripted lifelong adventure. They serve parents as fellow guides, graciously challenging moms and dads to walk closely with God beginning at home. Journeying Together is a creative, practical, and memorable resource that will prompt any family of disciples to grow in faith one step at a time.

 - Dan Lovaglia, Ministry Catalyst at Awana

Matt and his wife Noel have written a fun and creative devotional that every family should utilize. Using their personal experience as parents and children's pastors, they provide age appropriate devotionals that help children encounter God, unlike any other book.  - Dr. Chris Corbett, Professor of Religion at Southeastern University

Parents, your good intentions are not enough. You need to have an action plan to help your children love and follow God. There is no time to lose! Journeying Together is an action plan to help your children love God with all their hearts. It is doable, flexible, powerful, and fun!  - Dr. Rob Rienow, Founder of *Visionary Family Ministries*, www.VisionaryFam.com

# Table of Contents

## Part 3: Use Your Gear - Unpacking God's Gifts

## Part 4: Seek Shelter: Trusting God's Promises

# Introduction

**T**here's nothing like a true Adventure. A mountain hike with breathtaking views at the top. An underwater exploration teeming with creatures as mysterious as they are beautiful. A forest trek with winding paths that lead us deep into the unknown. Adventures teach us that preparation only gets us so far. Adventures show us that one step at a time takes us further from our comfort zone. Adventures open our eyes to the unknown, turning us into explorers who learn as we go along the way.

Parenting is a Daring Adventure. And like all adventures, it is as unpredictable as it is wondrous. We lead the way, onward and upwards, our children dependent on us to show them where to go. But at the end of this adventure, the hope is that our child will have everything they need to continue. If we guide them well, they will themselves become a guide on their own Daring Adventure someday, with their own children following behind. As Guides on this Daring Adventure, we may feel ill-equipped. The stakes are high, the risks are great, and it can be difficult to navigate in the dark.

We, like many parents, felt like faltering guides when our girls were small. We knew that passing on our faith was the most important part of our journey, but we struggled to do that well. We tried out different advice, but it felt like faulty equipment, and we couldn't seem to unpack it right. And then we were struck by the truth that WE aren't the Guides - God is. His spirit is with us, guiding us as we guide our children. So we began to focus less on plotting out our course and more on following the Spirit's prompting. We stopped using parenting books as our primary road maps and started following God's Word instead. I'd like to tell you our children have transformed into higher spiritual beings, but they are still just as sinful as the parents who passed on their sassy pants. We've had mountain top highs - moments when our kids experienced God in real, life-changing ways. And we've had deep valley lows - nights when we felt we'd led our child so far off course that we'd never find our way back. But while our Adventure sometimes veers off course, we have grown to know our Guide and trust his directions. And we invite you to do the same.

Think of this book not as a map, but as a travel journal, a place to stop and contemplate what God is doing on this adventure. Together we'll spend 52 weeks moving forward together, as we journey into deeper faith and trust in the God who guides us. We hope our vulnerability about our high and low points will connect with you and inspire you to keep moving. And we will always return to God's Word as the perfect answer to all of our questions, pointing to the God who walks with us always. Here's how this Adventure begins.

## SECTION ONE

# MEET YOUR GUIDE:
## Learning God's Names

We start at the beginning – by meeting our Guide. Learning who God is will take us a lifetime, but a great place to start is with his names. Throughout Scripture, we encounter different names for God, some used FOR God by his people, and others used by God to describe himself. These names help us connect with and relate to God as he guides us on our spiritual journey. While the English translations of the Bible are accurate and reliable, they often translate different names of God using God or Lord. Pay close attention so you can learn how to navigate these names as you read the Bible for yourself.

## SECTION TWO

# FOLLOW THE DIRECTIONS:
## Discovering God's Commands

We continue by studying what God values, as described by his commands to us, his followers. More than just a list of Shalls and Shalt Nots, these commands keep us on the straight and narrow path, safe from the pitfalls of veering off course. They also keep our hearts close to God, moving forward towards the final destination of our grand adventure – eternity spent with him.

## SECTION THREE

# USE YOUR GEAR:
# Unpacking God's Gifts

As we explore further, we'll take a look at the gifts God has given to enable us to experience and enjoy our journey thoroughly. These gifts give us the tools we need to not only keep moving on our spiritual journey but help others along the way as well. As we use our gear, putting these gifts to good use, we find purpose and meaning in the midst of our travels.

## SECTION FOUR

# SEEK SHELTER:
# Trusting God's Promises

Our journey wouldn't be complete without considering the harder parts of our journey – the rocky paths and passageways that are the result of a broken world. These difficult areas of the journey often make us want to run for cover, maybe even choose a less unrelenting path. But by knowing and trusting in God's promises, we can find shelter through the darkest of times, while staying the course and pursuing the adventure God has for us.

Throughout each devotional, you'll grow in your faith and find tangible ways to help your child grow in their faith as well. You'll journey through one devotional per week for 52 weeks, and at the end of your yearlong journey, you and your child will have adventures to celebrate, and stories to tell. There are four elements to each weekly devotional:

## MEDITATE

Passage of Scripture to read and for responding. This section will include a key passage of one or two verses, as well as a suggested extended passage for further study. Take time to not only read this passage each week but meditate on it, so its words will take root in your heart.

## ANTICIPATE

Reflection questions to help set the tone for the journey. These simple questions will prepare your heart and focus your thoughts so you can get ready to fully engage with God and your child. Take a few moments to reflect on these questions, examining your heart and answering transparently.

## RELATE

Honest stories from our parenting experiences, good and bad. These stories will remind you that we are all on this journey together. Often we compare ourselves with other parents at their best moment and feel ill-equipped for the journey ahead. Other times we witness setbacks and families who have lost their way and we worry that we don't stand a chance on such a narrow road. By sharing each others' stories and viewing them in the light of God's Word, we can find encouragement that we are not alone on the journey, and that together we can spur each other along the way.

# ON THE ROAD

An engaging application of the week's study for you to do with your child. There are four types of activities, designed to help you integrate your faith into the natural, everyday rhythms of your family life. These activities provide opportunities for you to create intentional space for God to guide you and your child into a deeper faith, and are based on Deuteronomy 6:7 "Impress them on your children. Talk about them when you sit at home, and when you walk along the road, when you lie down and when you get up." Rather than scrambling for extra time in your busy schedule, these activities will help you impress God's Word onto your children with the time that you've already been given.

## TIPS FOR Kids

Each week we will offer suggestions in these boxes to help your children learn the same truth you have been reflecting on that week. Here you will find age-appropriate ideas to help your preschooler and elementary-age child grow closer to God as you all journey down the same path together. Let the Journey into this Adventure begin.

## FAMILY Fun and CHAT Prompts

Each week find fun family activities and chat prompts for interactive ways to reinforce the learning with your children. Look for opportunities in the normal course of your week to talk together and enjoy the journey.

# CHAPTER 1

# Elohim

**MEDITATE**

*In the beginning, God created the heavens and the earth. Now the earth was formless and empty, darkness was over the surface of the deep, and the Spirit of God was hovering over the waters. And God said, "Let there be light," and there was light.* – Genesis 1:1-3

Extended passage: Genesis 1:1-31

**ANTICIPATE**

● What does wake up time look like at your house?

_____

_____

● How do you wake up every morning?

_____

_____

Waking up in the morning looks different at every age. As babies, children cry out in the night - alerting mom or dad to come and address a need. Waking up is initiated by the child during infant and toddler years because no one in their right mind would ever, EVER wake a sleeping child. All of that changes when your children start to attend preschool or elementary. The responsibility for beginning the day falls on parents. And here's where the fun begins.

## ALARM CLOCK

Using an alarm clock to wake up my children lacks both creativity and ingenuity. Once I needed to help my kids start the day, I tried some creative ploys. Kneeling next to them and patting their back, slowly leading them away from sleep. Walking into their room in a court jester costume and telling jokes. Playing "Good Morning" from Signing in the Rain and tap-dancing on the carpet. Releasing a younger sibling or pet in their room (or directly on their face). Placing smelly diapers next to their heads.

## IN THE BEGINNING

I told you this is fun. If I'm going to be responsible for starting my kid's day, I'm going to do something dramatic. And when I read Genesis 1:1, that's what God does. The very first sentence of the Bible is an introduction to the story, and it's primary character. "In the beginning God…" You may not realize that in the original language the Bible was written in, many names have been used for God and each one has a unique meaning. In Genesis 1:1, the name used is "Elohim." This name occurs 2600 times in Bible and speaks to the power and strength of God, which is on display throughout the rest Genesis 1 as the world is created. The use of the name "Elohim" is unique because while it is translated as God, "Elohim" is a plural word, meaning it covers more than one identity. Bible scholars have used this fact to show how the very first mention of God in the Bible gives us a picture of God as Father, Son, and Spirit. So even as the world is waking to life at the outset of the Bible, God reveals himself to be more than just a singular being but "Elohim."

**WAKE UP** God is the creator of the heavens and the earth. And we are part of his creation! This week, point your family to the beautiful truth that God made us and everything around us. By his voice, God spoke rivers and stars, mountains and valleys, birds and fish, zebras and alligators into existence.

## PRESCHOOL Kids

This week, wake your kids up by reading different verses from Genesis. On Monday, read Genesis 1:3 (on the first day). On Tuesday, read Genesis 1:4 ("on the second day…"), and repeat throughout the week. Remind your kids how God reveals himself through the creation story. Ask them, "What is God doing on this day of creation? What is created and how is it made?" Reflect together on God's creativity and power.

## FAMILY Fun

Go online and search for unique animals. Try and find animals, birds, or fish you have never seen before or have recently been discovered. Take time to explore these unique expressions of God's creative power. Ask your kids, "What do you notice about these creatures? How did God come up with so many different animals?"

## CHAT Prompts

Ask your child, "If you had the power to create anything, what would you make? What would it look like? What would it be able to do?"

# ELEMENTARY Kids

This week, wake your kids up in different ways. Get creative! Try reading verses from Genesis 1 in various voices. Cuddle them. Tickle them. Bring them breakfast. Or try a foghorn. Have fun with this! As you wake them up, ask: "What do you think it sounded like when God woke up the world? What did it look like? What happened?" As they go through their morning routine, prompt them to be mindful of God's creativity and power.

# CHAPTER 2

# El Shaddai

 **MEDITATE**

*Whoever dwells in the shelter of the Most High will rest in the shadow of the Almighty.* – Psalm 91:1

Extended passage: Psalm 91

 **ANTICIPATE**

● Recall a time when you felt overwhelmed and hopeless

_____

_____

● What does it look and feel like to truly be at rest?

_____

_____

## RELATE

We'd been hosting a little girl through Safe Families For Children for a few weeks, and it was time for her to return home. I packed and unpacked her bag, filling a smaller bag with essential items - a few warm outfits, socks and underwear, warm pajamas, her favorite stuffed animal - then a larger bag with extra clothes and toys. I showed her the bags and explained that the smaller bag was in case she needed to leave in an emergency. Last time she had packed too big of a bag, and since it was heavy, she had to leave it in an alley and keep moving somewhere safe. Packing up the bags is the hardest part of my job as a Safe Families mom. It's the last tangible thing I do for them, and as I pack their bags, it's hard not to imagine every difficult situation they may face. So I pack and then let go, trusting that when they leave our home, God will go with them.

## A LOVING GOD

Each of these children has loved hearing stories from the Bible. They cling desperately to the Truths they find in God's Word. It's easy to teach our children that we know God loves us because we have a warm house, plenty of food, parents that love and care for us. But for children who have known homelessness and hunger, who are loved by one family member but abused by another, they need assurances that God is loving and kind and strong even in the midst of their struggles.

## A PLACE TO REST

Psalm 91:1 promises that those who follow God will rest in the shadow of the Almighty, or El Shaddai. This name refers to God's omnipotence, his limitless power. Throughout Scripture, we see this power on display as God speaks the world into existence, parts the Red Sea, slays giants, and defeats Death itself. But here in Psalms, we read that God Almighty provides rest. Perhaps this seems like a trivial use of omnipotence. But if you've been a child on the run from danger that is all around, if you've found yourself in a dark place, overwhelming circumstances, unrelenting pain, rest is far beyond your reach unless God Almighty provides it with his very presence. El Shaddai reminds us that our all-powerful God is always near, and we can rest in his shadow.

# ON THE ROAD

**BEDTIME** After a busy day, our bodies need physical rest, but sometimes worry and stress can catch up to us, making it difficult to get the rest we need. Make bedtime a time where your child learns to rest in God's presence before they settle down to sleep.

## PRESCHOOL Kids

As you tuck your child into bed, share with them a favorite story from Scripture that demonstrates God's power. Explain that God is all-powerful – there is nothing he cannot do. Whatever worries or scares them is smaller than God. Tell them that God promises to give us rest in his shadow. Use your imaginations to picture what God's shadow might look like. Read Psalm 91:1 as a blessing over them before saying goodnight.

## FAMILY Fun

Plan some family "Rest Time." Cancel your plans in the middle of a busy week and spend an afternoon or evening doing something that feels "restful," whether it's playing board games, going for a long hike, or enjoying time at the beach. Afterward, talk about what it means for God to give us rest.

## CHAT Prompts

Is there a problem or worry that you're facing that feels huge right now? How can we pray for you?

## ELEMENTARY Kids

Before bed, ask your child if they can remember a story from Scripture that shows God's power, and then share your favorite story. Explain that God is omnipotent – this means he is all-powerful. There is nothing he cannot do! Share that he is bigger than their greatest problems or fears and that even when our problems or worries seem too big to handle, God promises to give us rest within his shadow. Ask your child what they think that means, to rest in God's shadow. Read Psalm 91:1 as a blessing over them before saying goodnight.

# CHAPTER 3

# Jehovah Shalom

## with Sofia Guevara

 **MEDITATE**

*So Gideon built an altar to the Lord there and called it The Lord Is Peace.* – Judges 6:24a

Extended passage: Judges 6:1-24

 **ANTICIPATE**

● What situations or problems are causing you to worry or be afraid?

_____

_____

● When have you experienced God's peace?

_____

_____

A few years ago, my sister Isabel was hospitalized. My parents stayed with Isabel in the hospital an hour and a half away while I stayed with my grandparents. Late that night, Isabel FaceTimed me. I was still awake, so worried that I could not sleep. I knew how much pain she was in when I saw her face. After the call, I was even more nervous. I asked my Grandma to pray for me, and after she had left, I heard a voice say, "Trust in the Lord. Then you will have peace." At that moment, I felt a sudden wave of peace wash over me. The next morning, I was rested and relaxed. God calmed my heart so I could learn to trust in him.

## DO NOT BE AFRAID

God came to Gideon during a difficult time. His people were oppressed and the God their parents had told them about seemed far off. They felt alone, deserted, afraid. Then the Lord appears and tells Gideon to go and save Israel but Gideon protests, asking God for a sign. The angel of the Lord appears, performs a miracle and then God speaks: "May peace be with you! Do not be afraid. You are not going to die." Gideon built an altar and called it "Jehovah Shalom," or The Lord is Peace.

## HE IS PEACE

I knew that night after talking with my sister that God had sent someone or something to remind me that peace will follow trust, just how after Gideon decided to trust God, he received peace. I had pondered what the Voice was, but when I read the story of Gideon, the idea popped into my head that it was an Angel of the Lord. In the midst of a difficult time, God showed me that He is Peace. Now whenever I am worried or afraid, I remind myself that God is with me and if I trust in him, he will give me peace.

**ON THE ROAD** Car rides are often stressful times – rushing from place to place, feeling the stress of running late and transitioning from one activity or place to the next can leave us feeling anxious. They are also a way to leave our worries and troubles behind physically. This time spent strapped into seats, in between point A and point B can offer an opportunity to put our trust in God and receive his peace. This week, make your time on the road a chance to trust in the God of Peace.

## PRESCHOOL Kids

When you buckle your child into their car seat, let them know that you are looking forward to this time in the car. Tell them the story of Gideon as you drive along the road, sharing how God helped Gideon by giving him peace. Ask your child what things they may be worried about or afraid of, and then invite them to pray with you that God will give them peace. Then turn on some music that will encourage you to trust in God and receive his peace.

## FAMILY Fun

Gideon built an altar to honor God and to be a reminder that God is peace. As a family, create your own "altar" – this could be a piece of art or a sculpture, anything that honors God and reminds you that God is peace. Display this "altar" somewhere in your home as a reminder to trust in God.

## CHAT **Prompts**

What are some ways we can remind ourselves to trust God when we feel worried or afraid? How can we make trusting God a habit in our home?

# ELEMENTARY **Kids**

As your child gets into the car, share how you want your time on the road to be a peaceful time. Tell them the story of Gideon as you are driving. Ask: how did God help Gideon? What does it look or feel like to have peace? Ask your child how you can be praying for them – what worries them or makes them anxious? Pray together that God will give them peace. Then turn on music that will focus your hearts on God's peace.

## CHAPTER 4

# YHWH

## MEDITATE

*Moses said to God, "Suppose I go to the Israelites and say to them, 'The God of your fathers has sent me to you,' and they ask me, 'What is his name?' Then what shall I tell them?" God said to Moses, "I am who I am. This is what you are to say to the Israelites: 'I am has sent me to you.'"*
— Exodus 3:13-14

Extended passage: Exodus 3:1-20

## ANTICIPATE

● What are some questions your mom or dad asked you repeatedly?

_____

_____

● What questions do you ask your child often?

_____

_____

My son Zion has given me the best answers to these questions. As you read these, picture a preschool boy answering with all sincerity.

Who do you think you are talking to? I'm talking to you Dad. You just asked me a question. And now, I'm giving the answer.

## BEST ANSWERS

Who do you think you are? Dad, I'm ZION!! REMEMBER?!? HOW COULD YOU FORGET YOUR SON!

What do you think you are doing? Dad, I just don't know.

## MOSES ASKS A QUESTION

What is remarkable about these questions is we find one of them in the Bible. Moses, having been visited upon by the angel of the Lord through a burning bush on the side of Mount Horeb, receives instructions to liberate the people of God. Moses is told to go to Egypt and command its leader to free the Israelites. And Moses asks God, ""Suppose I go to the Israelites and say to them, 'The God of your fathers has sent me to you,' and they ask me, 'What is his name?' Then what shall I tell them?" In other words, "Who do you think you are? I need to know because the Pharaoh is a pretty powerful guy – I spent years living with him – and he will want to know what he's really up against with this demand. I know he's going to ask who is behind all this."

## YHWH

And God replies, not with a title, but with his personal name, YHWH (or Yahweh). The name YHWH was respected, honored, and set apart that the Israelites never spoke it out loud. In your Bible, the name YHWH is translated as Lord, and it shows up nearly 7000 times. And in this proper name, we find the reality that God is real, existing forever with nothing before him or after him. While the world around us changes, God does not. He is YHWH, "I am who I am."

# ON THE ROAD

**AT HOME** Moms and Dads, while we face unique changes and challenges in our work, our home, or our children's behavior - YHWH is there. Maybe you have struggled, but your struggle did not exist before YHWH and will not outlast the Lord. He is constant. He is there. This week, spend time reflecting on the name of God and discussing names with your kids.

## PRESCHOOL Kids

Preschool children love names and naming things. At home this week, talk to your child about the names they have given to their toys, dolls, or stuffed animals. Share stories about names with them. Discuss where the nicknames come from you have given your children.

## FAMILY Fun

Our names reveal so much about us. Find what every name in your family means. Using a small framed chalkboard or a large poster, write down each family name with its meaning. Include God's name too! Hang this up in a prominent place in your house.

## CHAT **Prompts**

Read the story of Moses in Exodus 3 and highlight God's name. Practice using YHWH as you pray together with your child this week.

# ELEMENTARY **Kids**

Think about why you chose your child's name. What does their name mean? Do they share the same name as another family member? What was that person like? Think through the same questions for your name and discuss these things with your child. Read Exodus chapter 3 and talk about God's name. Have them find the places in the chapter where the word Lord has small capital letters. Ask your child, "What does God's name mean?"

# CHAPTER 5

# Adonai

 **MEDITATE**

*"Lord Almighty, God of Israel, you have revealed this to your servant, saying, 'I will build a house for you.' So your servant has found the courage to pray this prayer to you. Sovereign Lord, you are God! Your covenant is trustworthy, and you have promised these good things to your servant."* – 2 Samuel 7:27-28

Extended passage: 2 Samuel 7:18-29

 **ANTICIPATE**

● What famous stories do you cherish that you look forward to passing on to your children?

_____

_____

● What is the funniest thing your child has ever called you?

_____

_____

# RELATE

My son Zion loves Star Wars. It's a little odd because he has never seen the movies or cartoons yet he is familiar with the characters through film trailers, books, commercials, toys, and conversations with his big sisters, friends, and cousins. A mop, a hairdryer, even a bag of garbage can turn into a lightsaber. Zion talks about the characters like Luke Skywalker, Chewbacca, Kylo Ren, and the Emperor. Part of me cringes when this happens, mostly out of jealously because I had to wait 30 years to find out who Kylo Ren is and Zion is just a preschooler who hasn't even seen the movies! But there he goes, jumping off the walls and random furniture pretending to be a Jedi. The other day, Z came up to me and said, "Dad, you are my Jedi master. I am going to start calling you 'Master' now."

## MOMENTS

Now you know the greatest parenting moment I have ever experienced. And in this glorious moment, I encouraged my young Padawan learner and chose not to correct him. Parenting can be amazing sometimes.

## MY MASTER

While we do not find anything related to Jedi in the Bible, "Adonai" is a name for God that shows up often. Other words associated with Adonai according to Bible scholars include "Majesty," "Father," and (you guessed it) "Master." If you remember back to the devotional about YHWH, the proper name of God was so holy and set apart it was not spoken aloud. Instead, when God's people came across YHWH in the Bible, they used the name "Adonai," which is translated "Lord." So when you see the word Lord in the Bible without any small capital letters, you are reading some form of the name "Adonai."

## GOD REVEALS

Adonai is used hundreds of times in the Bible, including 2 Samuel 7 throughout a prayer of David. Having been called by God to build the temple, David prays "Lord Almighty, God of Israel, you have revealed this to your servant… Sovereign Lord, you are God!" (2 Samuel 7:28-29). Identifying God in this way is David's way of saying, "I will serve you Adonai, my Master. I will follow your instructions."

# ON THE ROAD

**BEDTIME** This week, take time before bedtime to reflect on the attitude of your heart. How are you showing reverence to and following God? How are your children honoring and responding to God?

## PRESCHOOL Kids

This week, play a game of Simon Says during bedtime. As you play the game, talk about the different roles you play. Say, "Let's play Simon Says. I am going to be Simon, and my job is to give you instructions. You are going to listen to my instructions. Only follow the instructions you hear after I say, 'Simon says.' Try different instructions like clapping, standing, rubbing your tummy, tickling your feet, or jumping on the bed. When you are done, talk about how in our lives God is the one who gives us instructions. He tells us how to live, and our job is to listen and obey his instructions.

## FAMILY Fun

Build something together. Find a building brick set or board game that requires you to follow instructions together. Have fun playing together! As you walk through the instructions, remind your kids that one of the names of God is Adonai, and God is the one who gives us instructions to follow for our lives.

## CHAT Prompts

One of God's names means "Master." What does a master look like to you? What does a master do? One of the responsibilities of a master is to give instructions. Where do we find God's instructions for us?

## ELEMENTARY Kids

During bedtime, set aside a moment to give God honor. Talk to your child about what it means to honor someone. Ask, "How would you honor someone who deserved it? What does it look like to honor another person?" When we give God honor, we show God how much we respect him and how we understand that he is in charge. Pray together and use different words to honor God for who he is and what he has done.

# CHAPTER 6

# Jehovah-Rapha

*with Isabel Guevara*

 **MEDITATE**

*Praise the Lord, my soul, and forget not all his benefits—who forgives all your sins and heals all your diseases, who redeems your life from the pit and crowns you with love and compassion, who satisfies your desires with good things so that your youth is renewed like the eagles.*

*- Psalm 103:2-5*

Extended passage: Psalm 103:1-22

 **ANTICIPATE**

● Have you ever witnessed a miracle? What happened?

_____

_____

● What is the worst sickness you've ever faced?

_____

_____

## RELATE

Guess what? Everyone wants to witness a miracle – to see a miraculous display of God's power or to experience something supernatural. But no one wants to need a miracle. When I was ten years old, I needed a miracle. I woke up one morning unable to move my legs. For months, I struggled to walk to the point where I needed to borrow my great-grandmother's walker, complete with frayed green tennis balls stuck to the legs. I promise, no ten-year-old girl is dreaming of the day she can go to school with a walker. Stairs became my archenemy. The pain my constant companion.

## THE MYSTERY

We tried everything to solve the mystery behind the pain. Doctors. Blood tests. X-rays, and an MRI. No one could help me get well. I prayed. I pleaded with God by myself and with my family. I asked friends, teachers, and church leaders to pray for me too. Months passed, and nothing changed. I was still living the dream of a ten-year-old granny walker auditioning for the role of Quasimodo.

## MIRACLE

My grandparents attended a church that held special prayer meetings for people who needed to be healed. After a year of unbearable pain, I wanted to be healed. My dad and I came to the prayer service, and while many of the details escape me, I left the prayer meeting walking straight and without any pain. I experienced a miracle.

## JEHOVAH RAPHA

One of the names of God is "Jehovah Rapha" which is translated as the "God who heals." Rapha is a Hebrew word meaning, "to restore" or "to bring back to health." And there are so many examples of God as Jehovah Rapha restoring people from the disease of sin in Psalms, Isaiah, and Jeremiah. The Gospels are filled with accounts of Jesus touching sick people with his hands to bring them back to health. Healing is not a magic power of our God, it is part of his character to restore and redeem, and we need his healing more than anything in our lives. Our sins have moved us far from his side, but through Jehovah Rapha, we are restored.

# ON THE ROAD

**AT HOME**  When you restore a piece of furniture or a car, you are taking something old, broken, and worn out and making it new once again. Restoration is the work of Jehovah Rapha, a healing God. And in the work of parenting, we can become run down, tired, even broken. Did you know God sees all of it and has the capacity, power, and desire to restore you and bring you back to health? This week, consider what needs to be restored and healed in your life. Submit these things to Jehovah Rapha.

## PRESCHOOL Kids

Invite your child to help you with a special project. Gather some pieces of scrap paper - construction paper, scrapbook paper, or even tissue paper will do, then rip them up into pieces. Explain that these papers were once new and all in one piece, but now they seem ruined. Invite your child to help you glue the pieces onto a new piece of paper to make something new. Once your project is finished, admire how beautiful it is and remind your child that God is our healer and restorer.

### FAMILY Fun

Find an old piece of furniture (look in your basement or garage) and paint it with your family. Don't have one around the house? Keep your eye out on trash day or at local garage sales. Furniture like this is often thrown away. With some cheap paint and elbow grease, restore it and be reminded of how God makes us new.

## CHAT Prompts

Talk about God's healing power.
Has God ever healed you?
Have you ever seen God heal
someone else?

# ELEMENTARY Kids

Take some focused time to pray with your child this week.
Before starting this time of prayer, read Psalm 103. Ask
your child, "Is there anyone we can pray for who is sick
and needs God to heal them?" Pray for each person
by name and ask God to do all of the things you read
about in the Psalm. Remind your child to keep praying
throughout the week.

**CHAPTER 7**

# El Roi

*She answered God by name, praying to the God who spoke to her, "You're the God who sees me! "Yes! He saw me, and then I saw him!"*
— Genesis 16:13 MSG

Extended passage: Genesis 16, 19:9-21

● What makes it difficult for you to pay attention to your child(ren)?

_____

_____

● Have you ever felt invisible? How did that feel?

_____

_____

## RELATE

Growing up with siblings means that you share the spotlight, sometimes competing for your parents' attention, sometimes deflecting their surveillance. No matter how hard I try to give equal amounts of love and attention to each of my four children, most days I fall short, and my kids are quick to remind me. "Moooommm, did you hear my question/see my ninja moves/get the supplies for my project?" The truth is, I don't always hear/see/respond to my children when they call. Some days I'm a multitasking ninja, and other days I stumble around with cold coffee and pathetically slow reflexes.

### BEING INVISIBLE

It's frustrating to feel unheard, unseen, ignored. But while my children may have to wait their turn, they are cherished and receive plenty of love and attention. Hagar, on the other hand, knows what it means to be truly alone. We find her pregnant and on the run from an abusive mistress, slavery behind her and nothing but desert stretched ahead. I struggle with the injustice of this story; I want something better for Hagar, I expect something different from Sarai and Abraham. But Scripture always points us to God and here we turn to find a God who has not abandoned Hagar. In fact, he has sought her out, there in the desert, in the midst of her despair.

### WHAT WE NEED

And there in the desert, God speaks to Hagar. I get hung up on the message - why would God tell her to go back, what hope is hidden in the promise? But Hagar's response brings me back to what matters: "You're the God who sees me!" She uses the name El Roi, a name not used anywhere else in Scripture. The next verse tells us that God not only saw her but revealed himself to her - she saw God. While I seek justice for Hagar, she found what she needed in El Roi, the God who saw her, and the God who was seen by her. This God is still the God who sees - he still seeks us out and reveals himself to us. And in our mostly lonely, difficult moments, El Roi is all we need.

**AT HOME** Children don't typically enjoy being alone and are often impatient when waiting for Mom or Dad to respond to them. As they get older facing conflict at school or even at home may make them feel alone. It is important to teach them from an early age that God always sees them. Playing a game of Hide and Seek is a fun way to illustrate how God will always seek us out and make himself known.

## PRESCHOOL Kids

Invite your child to play a game of Hide and Seek. Tell them to find a really good hiding spot, then wait for you to come and find them. Count to ten, then set off to find your child. When you do find them, say, "I found you! Now I can see you, and you can see me, too!" Remind your child that God can always see them, and they are never alone.

## FAMILY Fun

Stand with your child in front of a mirror. Tell them what you see – begin with physical attributes, and then move on to what you see inside of your child. Call out the things you see and admire about their character, their heart, and their potential.

## CHAT **Prompts**

When was a time you felt like no one was listening to you or noticing you? How did it feel? What things would you most like me to notice about you?

# ELEMENTARY **Kids**

Ask your child to play a game of Hide and Seek – older children may enjoy playing in the dark or even outside. Challenge your child to find a great hiding spot, then wait for you to come and find them. Count to ten (or higher) and then seek out your child. When you find them, yell, "I see you!" Repeat the game a few times then ask your child if they have ever felt alone or like no one noticed them. Tell your child that God always sees them, and he will seek them out just like you did during the game. Remind them that whenever they feel alone, they can trust in God who sees them and wants them to know he is with them.

# CHAPTER 8

# El Chaiyai

## MEDITATE

*Deep calls to deep in the roar of your waterfalls; all your waves and breakers have swept over me. By day the Lord directs his love, at night his song is with me—a prayer to the God of my life.* – Psalm 42:7-8

Extended passage: Psalm 42:1-11

## ANTICIPATE

● What modes of travel do you most enjoy?

_____

_____

● Describe the worst travel moment you've ever experienced.

_____

_____

# RELATE

Several years ago, my family saved for months so we could attend my brother's graduation from college in Sydney, Australia. With as many family members as possible, we trekked to Australia and rented a house in Manly, a beautiful city across the bay from Sydney. The fastest and cheapest way to cross the bay each day for sightseeing was to take a ferry. Now, I am not a big fan of boats. Pirates would refer to me as a "landlubber." The thought of being on a ship for any reason makes me cringe. And the Manly Ferry route to Circular Quay (pronounced "Key") traverses the spot where the heads of the South Pacific Ocean roll into the bay. The trip gets a little choppy (and by choppy I mean, "batten down the hatches").

## LOSING THE HORIZON

One of these ferry trips was particularly terrifying to me. The water was already rough, and as we sailed to the ocean heads, the ferry began to lose the horizon in all directions. We tipped forward, and we rolled sideways, and I panicked. I froze in my seat, unable to move or speak. Meanwhile, the rest of my family is sitting outside the boat so they can take in all the action. And I hear my sweet daughters teasing me, "Dad's going to puke! He should sit out here so he can just lean over the side of the boat. Easy cleanup!" I was tempted to throw them overboard. Thankfully I was unable to move my arms.

## GOD OF MY LIFE

Psalm 42 is a song about waves that overwhelm. It was written by the sons of Korah, a group of leaders charged with the ministry of singing in the Tabernacle. This song is a personal chorus speaking directly to God. Note how the writers use the words "your waves" and "your breakers" and they address the one who sent the waves and breakers uniquely as "God of my life" or "El Chaiyai" (emphasis mine). This psalm is the only place in the Bible where this name of God is used. I find it amazing how the sovereign God over all creation, the eternal Lord of heaven, can be over everything and yet be personally connected to me. How is this possible for the King above all other Kings know the most intimate details of every person in the kingdom?

# ON THE ROAD

**WAKE UP** Moms and Dads, our hope is in a personally connected God. This truth is the ballast in our little parenting boat of faith. The most important thing you can teach your children is to recognize and trust in God over their life. So this week, have conversations with your child about trusting God in this way and call on him.

## PRESCHOOL Kids

Has your preschooler made a decision to respond to the truth of God's Story and the sacrifice of Jesus on the cross? Have they called out to God to save them from their sin? If not, this week is an incredible week to have this conversation. From the moment they wake up, let them know just how much God loves them. Watch a video on Youtube about Jesus's life, death, and resurrection during breakfast. Emphasize how this was all because God wants to be their God. Help them to repent of their wrong choices and express their belief in God.

## FAMILY Fun

Learn to pronounce this name of God, El Chaiyai ("El Cay-yigh"). Go back to previous chapters and try to pronounce the different names of God.

## CHAT Prompts

What is shaking you right now? What has you uncertain? Are you worried about anything right now? Pray together and give those things to God.

# ELEMENTARY Kids

Has your child made a decision to put their faith and trust in God? One morning this week, read some of these Bible verses together: Romans 3:23, Romans 6:23, John 3:16, and Romans 10:13. After each reading, ask "What do you notice about this verse? What is God saying?" Help them articulate what God has done for them.

# CHAPTER 9

# El Olam

## MEDITATE

*Trust in the Lord forever, for the Lord, the Lord himself is the Rock eternal.* – Isaiah 26:4

Extended passage: Isaiah 26

## ANTICIPATE

● What do you struggle to trust God with?

_____

_____


● What comes to mind when you think of God as Eternal or Everlasting?

_____

_____

We'd been through a lot of changes in recent months - welcomed a baby, lost a foster child, moved homes, schools, and jobs - and our girls had managed those transitions with grace. We decided to leave baby Zion with his grandma and set off for a Colorado adventure with Isabel and Sofi. They were captivated by the mountains. We took a train up to Pike's Peak, and as we stood at the top, my eyes scanned the view that stretched for miles in all directions. I saw the world differently, less focused on what was right at my fingertips and more focused on what stretched out before me. I marveled at the mountains' permanence - the way they stood firm and unshakeable throughout time. While our world had been upended, they had continued to stand tall as they always have. As they always will.

## SONG OF PRAISE

Isaiah writes his book of prophecy in an upended world. He speaks on God's behalf of devastation and destruction, of nations that stand strong, but will soon collapse. It's the kind of book you want to skim through to find the happy ending at the end. And here in the middle, Isaiah's Song of Praise ushers me to stop right here and set my mind on God. Trust in El-Olam, "The Everlasting God." The God who is Eternal - who always was and always will be. God himself is everlasting, but who God is - his character - is also everlasting. Unchanging. Without beginning or end. Eternal.

## PARENTING FOR ETERNITY

When my world is upended and shaken, I need an everlasting God. But in my everyday life, I need him, too. As a mom, I often focus on the Right Now. I wake up and hit the ground running; today's To Do List my task master. But while those things are important today, the souls in my care were created by an Everlasting God. These days are long but these years are moving quickly, and if I am to pass on faith in an Everlasting God, I must live and parent with my mind set on him. This Everlasting God like the Colorado mountain beneath me is firm, secure, unshakeable, and he sets my eyes on eternity stretched before me.

# ON THE ROAD

**ON THE ROAD** The eternal and everlasting nature of God is difficult for adults to grasp, but children have much to teach us about faith, often more willing to believe in a God they don't understand. This week, point them to the Everlasting God and allow yourself to learn from their childlike faith.

## PRESCHOOL Kids

Take your child out somewhere open and quiet one evening to star gaze. As you look up at the vastness of the heavens, talk about how God spoke the stars into existence long before you were born. But even before the stars, God existed. Read Isaiah 26:4 and share that we can trust in God, who always was and always will be. Invite your child to share their thoughts on God. Ask what they think God is like, what it means that God always was and always will be, why trusting in God is so important. Before you leave, sing a song of praise like Isaiah to the Everlasting God.

## FAMILY Fun

Go on a hike together. Acting as Guide, invite your child to follow you and trust you to lead them. When you reach your destination, remind your child that God is not only our Guide, but the Everlasting God, and he wants to show us the way to live with him forever.

## CHAT **Prompts**

If you knew that you would live forever, what would you do with your life?

# ELEMENTARY **Kids**

Invite your child out on a stargazing adventure. Drive out to somewhere open and quiet, and talk about what you see in the sky on the way. Discuss how old the stars are, and how God created them long before anyone on the earth was born. Ask your child what it means that God is Eternal. Read Isaiah 26:4 and ask your child how they picture God. Discuss why it's important to put our trust in God. Before you leave, take a cue from Isaiah and sing a song of praise to the Everlasting God.

# CHAPTER 10

# Shepherd

## MEDITATE

*The Lord is my shepherd; I lack nothing. He makes me lie down in green pastures; he leads me beside quiet waters, he refreshes my soul. He guides me along the right paths for his name's sake.*

– Psalm 23:1-3

Extended passage: Psalm 23:1-6

## ANTICIPATE

● What was your favorite subject in grade school?

_____

_____

● Are you a leader or a follower?

_____

_____

# RELATE

Do you remember math in grade school? Multiplication facts. Long division. Fractions. All the stuff of every child's dreams. As a student, I loathed math. I would read word problems like, "The track at Joan's school is a 1/2 mile long. Joan ran 15/16 of the length of the track. How many feet did Joan run?" And I would think, "Do us all a favor Joan and JUST FINISH THE LAST SIXTEENTH OF A MILE. " Because you're wondering, the answer is "Ask Siri."

## LEARNING TO THINK

My distaste for math notwithstanding, I use math every single day in my job and over the years I became the in-home math tutor for my kids. My daughter Isabel has struggled with math from time to time. But as I sat down with her to walk through measurements, drawing lines, and determining angles I discovered that Isabel's problem was not in understanding math but in going too fast. Isabel wants to get an answer down on paper as quickly as possible so she can spend less time on math. This habit causes her to take shortcuts like guessing or not reading directions. And as I worked with her time and time again, my goal was to teach her math and get her to think, not get right answers every time.

## THE GUIDANCE WE NEED

This careful, guiding leadership is reminiscent of the job of a shepherd. In the modern world, the task of a shepherd does not often show up on a Facebook of a LinkedIn profile. A shepherd's job is to take care of sheep, to lead the herd where they need to go. Sheep are not known for their intuition or sense of direction. They would wander aimlessly without a guide. In Psalm 23, David famously refers to the Lord as a shepherd who guides, leads, and directs. What an incredible picture of God. Moms and dads, we often lose our way as parents. We do not make the best choices; we get off course, we may even try to take shortcuts, so things are a little easier in our home. The guidance of a shepherd is what we need each day.

# ON THE ROAD

**CAR TIME** If the Lord is our shepherd, the question for you and me is: will we follow? As a dad, I have a picture of where I want to be in 5 years and what I want for my family. Will I follow the Lord if his plan is different from my own? Will I trust him to take my family where we need to be? A wise pastor once told me, "watch how people follow." This week, get to know the Lord, your shepherd. Where is God taking you and your family? Where is he leading, guiding, and directing your journey?

## PRESCHOOL Kids

Drive to a park and lead your preschooler on a walk. Take lots of turns. Say, "We're going for a walk, and I need you to follow me no matter what." Reinforce how God leads us like a shepherd leads his sheep.

### FAMILY Fun

Just for fun, pick an evening and put on some lively music. Start a conga line with your family! As you dance through your house or living room, give each family member a chance to lead the line.

## CHAT Prompts

Talk to your child about what they want to be when they grow up. Ask, "Is God leading you to fulfill a big dream with your life? Where do you think God is taking you? How will you follow God's direction as you get older?"

# ELEMENTARY Kids

At some point this week, when you can get into the car a few minutes early, let you child navigate the car ride to a familiar place. Say, "I'm going to drive us today, but you get to tell me how to get there. You tell me when to turn and when to keep going straight. I'm going to follow your lead." As you make your way to your destination, talk about how Shepherd is one of the names of God. A Shepherd directs his sheep to the places they need to go for food and water and rest. Ask, "How is a shepherd leading his sheep similar to the way you are guiding us to where we are going?"

**CHAPTER 11**

# El Emet

MEDITATE

*Into Your hand I commit my spirit; You have ransomed me, Oh Lord, God of truth.* – Psalm 31:5

Extended passage: Psalm 31

ANTICIPATE

● How would you define truth?

_____

_____

● What Truths do you place your trust in?

_____

_____

Sofi's first-grade teacher asked the class if they had done anything fun or interesting over Spring Break. She waited her turn, then shared the exciting details of her surprise hot air balloon ride. Her friends were impressed. She couldn't wait to tell me all about it when she came home. The only problem was, she never took a hot air balloon ride. This detail seemed unimportant to a six-year-old who thought the point of story time was simply to tell the best story, regardless of whether or not it was true.

## WHAT IS TRUTH?

A six-year-old has a shaky standard of truth; they are still learning what truth is. In a culture that sells distorted versions of truth in commercials, celebrity social media accounts, and viral videos, it's easy to forget that Truth is firm, unwavering, unshakable. But our children desperately need Truth as a compass to set their hearts on the right path. David knew this all too well, and he writes Psalm 31 as a prayer for deliverance. He had powerful enemies who lied and plotted and conspired against him; even his friends bought the lies and abandoned him. His circumstances dire, he chose to put his trust in God, whom he calls El Emet or "faithful God of Truth." I find it interesting that he didn't seek help from the "God of Justice," or "God of Protection." He placed his hope, his very life, into the hands of the God who is Truth.

## FIRM AND FAITHFUL

The word *Emet* is similar to the the Hebrew word for Amen, which means firm and faithful. It is used at the end of prayers to confirm the words that were spoken. Amen is a firm and faithful response to a firm and faithful God. *El Emet* holds us up when everything around is uncertain, He never lies or fails to keep his promises. As parents, it is our job to point our children to the Faithful God of Truth and to eagerly learn what his Word says so that he can guide us along the right path.

# ON THE ROAD

Children often struggle with the abstract concept of Truth – they may know the difference between a truth and a lie, but what about make-believe, exaggeration, secrets, stories, and half-truths? We can't sort these nuances out in one sitting; we can teach our children that truth is firm and faithful. Together, build a fort to explore why we need a firm and faithful God of Truth.

## PRESCHOOL Kids

Tell your child that you would like to build a fort together. Once you've gathered sheets and blankets, begin throwing them up in the air, showing frustration that they aren't turning into a fort. Toss a corner over a chair and scratch your head when the "fort" collapses. Ask for your child's help, and together, discover that your fort needs something firm – like a book or a weight – to make it secure. Share that God is Truth. He is always firm and faithful; he never lets us down.

### FAMILY Fun

Play "2 Truths and a Lie." List three "facts" about yourself and see if your kids can guess which one is a lie. Discuss how sometimes a lie can be convincing, and that when we listen to the God of Truth, he will show us the right path.

## CHAT **Prompts**

Has someone ever lied to you?
Has someone ever made a
promise and then let you down?
How did that make you feel?

# ELEMENTARY **Kids**

Invite your child to help you build a fort using only sheets
and blankets. If they protest, ask them what else they
would need and why. Include their suggestions and work
together to make a more secure fort. Point out that your
fort needed something firm – furniture to prop up the
bedding, books to hold them in place. Without these
things, your fort would collapse. Share that God is Truth
and that he is always firm and faithful – more than furniture
and weights. He holds us up and never lets us down.

**CHAPTER 12**

# Jehovah Jireh

**MEDITATE**

*So Abraham named that place The Lord Will Provide. To this day people say, "It will be provided on the mountain of the Lord."*

– Genesis 22:14 (NIRV

Extended passage: Genesis 22:1-19

**ANTICIPATE**

● What does it mean to you that God sees you?

_____

_____

● What do you struggle to trust God with?

_____

_____

# RELATE

I was in the house while the girls were playing on their playset in the backyard. One minute I heard laughter, the next minute I heard screams. I didn't see Isabel fall, but as I opened the screen door I saw her face, and without thinking, I ran to her. I scooped her up and carried her back in the house, despite the fact that I was pregnant and her eight-year-old frame was much heavier than the last time I had tried to lift it. As a parent we know this: when we see our child in need, we respond. Whether it's to rescue them after a fall or correct them when we see them veering off course, to see is to respond.

## ABRAHAM'S JOURNEY

Abraham must have known this feeling. Blessed with a son in his old age, he undoubtedly cherished his boy, and he raised him to know and love the One True God. God had promised this son to Abraham, and he had fulfilled that promise miraculously. And yet here Abraham was, being asked by God to sacrifice this promised son. That trek up the mountain must have been excruciating, and while I have to imagine Abraham had his doubts, he was willing to trust God and respond with obedience. Then with knife raised and Isaac's life hanging in the balance, God calls Abraham by name, and spares his son, providing a ram for the sacrifice instead.

## PROVIDES AND SEES

Abraham's response is to name the place Jehovah Jireh, or The Lord Will Provide. The Hebrew translates more literally to "The Lord Will See." So how did we get from "see" to "provide?" The Story of Redemption, woven throughout Scripture, points us to a God who sees and then acts. This God who set the world in motion does not passively stand by and watch it spin on its axis. He does not sit on high and observe our comings and goings, detached from our triumphs and our struggles. He sees, and he responds, he moves on our behalf, he provides what he knows we need. This interconnection of seeing and acting is who God is. Jehovah Jireh sees you and provides what you need at the moment that you need it.

**WAKE UP** The hour or so after your child wakes up is often spent meeting their needs in rapid succession. These tasks are an opportunity to teach our child that we see their needs and respond. This week, use this first hour of the morning to show your child that just like you see them and provide for them, their Heavenly Father sees and provides for them, too.

## PRESCHOOL Kids

Wake your child up and say, "Good morning! It's so good to see you!" As you continue through your morning routine, verbalize what you see and how you act ("I see you need help with your shoes and I'd be happy to provide help and tie them for you"). When you have a quiet moment with your child, let them know that you love to see them and provide help when they need it. God is our perfect provider – he sees us all the time, and he will provide what he knows we need.

## FAMILY Fun

Gather as a family and talk about what you need - things you trust in God to provide. Write these things down on notecards, place them in a spot you'll see them, and commit to praying for them together every day. Trust that God sees your needs and is already at work, providing you with exactly what he knows you need.

## CHAT Prompts

As a family, discuss times that God has provided for you. How did he see and act? Did he provide for you in a way that you expected?

# ELEMENTARY Kids

As you wake your child up, greet them cheerfully and let them know you're so happy to see them. Throughout your morning routine, state what you see and how you act. ("I see you're hungry, I'm happy to provide you with breakfast.") When things are less hectic, let your child know that when you see them, you can't help but respond – providing help, course correction, or just a hug. Let them know that God always sees us, and it is in his character to respond. He is our perfect provider, always seeing us and providing what he knows we need.

## CHAPTER 13

# Immanuel

**MEDITATE**

*All this took place to fulfill what the Lord had said through the prophet: "The virgin will conceive and give birth to a son, and they will call him Immanuel" (which means "God with us").* – Matthew 1:22-23

Extended passage: Matthew 1:18-24

**ANTICIPATE**

● What place do you most enjoy being with your child?

_____

_____

● What do you enjoy doing together?

_____

_____

During the years I spent serving in the church as a children's pastor, I worked every weekend, so Fridays were my day off. When Isabel and Sofia were in Kindergarten and 1st grade, I would routinely visit their school on Fridays. Sometimes I would volunteer in their classroom for a party or help with a project. If there was a field trip on a Friday, I wanted to be there. But my favorite thing to do was visit during lunch.

## THE LUNCH ROOM

Lunch with kindergarteners and 1st graders is downright hilarious. A visiting parent is an instant celebrity. The parent, who is visiting is treated like royalty. It is the best experience, especially if you bring McDonalds with you. I loved sitting at the lunch table because I could hear funny stories about the class, teachers, and the kids' families. They would ask me questions like, "What do you do?" and I would always come up with something outrageous like "I'm an astronaut in a secret space program" or "I'm a magician whose main trick is to guess children's names and ages." (In these grades, they just did not possess the understanding that everyone in the class is pretty much the same age.) I asked my daughters what their favorite part of school lunch with dad was and their answer surprised me. It was the simple fact that I showed up. Not the celebrity status. Not the jokes. Not the McDonalds. Just me being with them.

## THE SHINING LIGHT OF PRESENCE

One of the most beautiful names of God is Immanuel. It means, "God with us." We know this name because it shows up in the Christmas season. We read the name in the prophecy of Isaiah and see it fulfilled in the Gospel of Matthew. Immanuel is more than the reality that God put on flesh but that he came to earth to be with his creation. The presence of God in his story sets the story apart from all other stories. And the name Immanuel reminds us that regardless of our situation, we are never without hope. This name of God is a shining light in the darkness of uncertainty and fear. For our God is always with us.

# ON THE ROAD

**WAKE UP** God's presence is the whole point of his story. And in children's lives, our presence as moms and dads is vital. But Houston, we have a problem. The largest distraction for most parents (including me) is their smartphone. We can do better, and our children will notice the difference. This week, remove distractions so you can be with your child.

## PRESCHOOL Kids

Create a moment just to be with your preschooler. Let them know you are so excited to spend time with them! Ask your child, "What's your favorite thing to do?" Is there a toy, game, or book they love to read? Let them know you would like to spend time doing their favorite thing. As you spend time together, say, "You are my child, and I am so happy to be with you. And God loves to be with his children too."

### FAMILY Fun

Plan a surprise visit to your child's school for lunch or a school event. This surprise will make their day. Let them know just how important they are for you to spend time with.

## CHAT Prompts

Read the story of the angel Gabriel talking to Mary and Joseph in Matthew chapter 1. Why is the name Immanuel important?

# ELEMENTARY Kids

Older children are more independent, but they still enjoy it when their parents spend time with them. Let your child know that you would like to just spend time with them. As you prepare for this time, ask your child what they would like to do together. Take note of their interests and find out why they enjoy that activity. Let your child know you are so glad to be able to just be with them. Tell them, "God loves to be with us too, it's why he is called "Immanuel."

# CHAPTER 14

# No gods Before Me

## MEDITATE

*Do not put any other gods in place of me.* – Exodus 20:3 (NIRV)

Extended passage: Psalm 145 (NIRV)

## ANTICIPATE

- What was on your To-Do list today and how do those things align with your priorities?

_____

_____

- How do you put God first in your life? How are you teaching your child to do the same?

_____

_____

I grew up in a non-denominational church, and while we celebrated Easter, I knew little of Lent. As an adult, I have incorporated some Lenten traditions in our home - this year we ate Pacskis on Fat Tuesday. I didn't say all of the traditions are spiritual. I think we can all agree that pastries deserve their place on the calendar. This Easter, I was reading a devotional that focused on Lent and decided to follow a similar reading plan with Zion using a children's Bible. I was writing the daily reading on our calendar and explaining how we'd place a sticker on the calendar each day after reading the Bible story all the way to Easter. I paused - "Zion, do you remember Easter?" To which he replied, "Yes! Yes, I remember Easter, I love Easter! It's when we celebrate Jesus and how he was crucified, buried, and then rose again on the third day!"

Ok, maybe I made up that last part. I'm pretty sure Zion answered, "It's when we find the eggs!!!!" Parent fail.

## FIRST THINGS FIRST

God's first Command is a call to keep God first. Above all else. Before all others. In a culture that's fast-paced and driven, a dozen things are competing for the #1 spot in our hearts, calendars, and to-do list at any given moment. We struggle to balance work and family, and as a parent, we are always scrambling to manage our kids' behavior, tend to their hearts, support their interests, encourage their talents, celebrate their successes, cultivate their character in this window of opportunity that we have to prepare our children for adulthood, teaching them this command of putting God first sometimes falls by the wayside. Even in our home.

## ALWAYS ENOUGH

But this first command paves the way for all the rest. My twelve-year-old daughter explained it this way: "When other things come first, you just want them more, and more but you're never happy because they're never enough. When God comes first, the more you want of him, the more he gives, so you always have enough." Maybe I'm not failing after all.

**WAKE UP** Children are often very literal, so teaching them first thing in the morning to talk to God is a great way to teach them to put God first in their lives. This week, begin each morning with a simple blessing.

## PRESCHOOL Kids

When you wake your preschooler up each morning, read Psalm 145:1-2 (NIRV) as a blessing over them, and then model a simple prayer thanking God for who he is and what he has done. Invite your child to pray their own prayer. Then remind your child that when God is #1 in our life, we have everything we need.

### FAMILY Fun

Encourage each person in your family to put God first by setting aside time each day to read God's Word. This time doesn't have to be a long and formal process, especially for your younger child. Focus on teaching your child to put God first by making time in his Word a priority.

## CHAT Prompts

What things, activities, or people are really important to you? Do those things always make you happy? How do they sometimes disappoint you or not seem like enough?

# ELEMENTARY Kids

When you wake your child up each morning, read Psalm 145:1-2 (NIRV) as a blessing over them.

Then encourage your child to take the next step by making it a  habit talking with God each morning. If they are unsure how to do this, pray with them – either have them repeat after you or take turns thanking God for simple things like their favorite toy, a beautiful day, special friends and family. Remind your child that God is the most important, and when he comes first, we always have enough.

**CHAPTER 15**

# You Shall Not Make An Idol

**MEDITATE**

*You shall not make for yourself an image in the form of anything in heaven above or on the earth beneath or in the waters below. You shall not bow down to them or worship them; for I, the Lord your God, am a jealous God, punishing the children for the sin of the parents to the third and fourth generation of those who hate me, but showing love to a thousand generations of those who love me and keep my commandments.* – Exodus 20:4-6

Extended passage: Psalm 115:1-8

**ANTICIPATE**

● How do your kids interact with social media?

_____

_____

● In 10 words or less, what do you want most in your life?

_____

_____

## RELATE

One morning as my daughters were getting ready for school, Sofia asked me to take their picture. I grabbed my phone and snapped a quick photo. Sofia immediately told me, "Put the picture on Facebook. I want to see how many likes we get!"

## BLOW-DRIED PERFECTION

Social media has made parenting much more difficult because we can see the picture-perfect lives of others and we strive to replicate it. And our children notice. There's something about witnessing this blow-dried perfection on daily display that puts us as parents into an all-out sprint to overdo everything. It is seeing the themed bedrooms, the themed vacations, even the themed pancakes. We're theming pancakes now! Listen, if being a good parent has anything to do with making themed pancakes, I am not going to win parenting ever.

## IDOL WORSHIP

The second commandment given to Moses is simple. Do not make any idols. Back in the time of ancient Israel, it was easy to identify people by the carving they worshiped. From Egypt to Mesopotamia there were Baals and Asherahs and sculpted images of animals and pharaohs. An idol was an easy thing to identify. Now when we think of idols as the image of a resting Buddha or the various Hindu gods may come to mind. But idol worship is not about getting your tools out and carving a log into an elephant for the altar you set up in your basement. Idolatry is about anything you worship. And nothing could be more important because you become like what you worship.

## WHAT WE WORSHIP

King David writes in Psalm 115:4-8, "But their idols are silver and gold, made by human hands. They have mouths, but cannot speak, eyes, but cannot see. They have ears, but cannot hear, noses, but cannot smell. They have hands, but cannot feel, feet, but cannot walk, nor can they utter a sound with their throats. Those who make them will be like them, and so will all who trust in them." What we worship changes us and when we stir our affections towards other things and replace the pursuit and love of God with those things, we violate the second commandment.

# ON THE ROAD

**CAR TIME** Scripture tells us God is a jealous God. He not only deserves all our attention, all our affection, and all our heart – he is jealous for them. And I think we can admit the idols we worship in God's place pale in comparison, yet they are so easy to worship. Entertainment. Money. Successful children. Admiration. This week, make car time all about discussing the things you pay attention to the most. Consider how those things might be replacing God.

## PRESCHOOL Kids

As you ride in the car this week, talk about important things in your child's life. What do they enjoy doing? What do they spend lots of time doing? Use the things you see on your drive as prompts. As you drive past an athletic store, talk about sports. As you drive past a grocery store, talk about food. As you drive past an electronics store, talk about video games or television. Tell your preschooler, "Sometimes we can make things so important to us, we start to pay more attention to them than we do to God. God wants us to give him all of our heart, and he tells us not to worship anything else."

## FAMILY Fun

Make a top ten list together! As a family, brainstorm the ways you can protect your heart from worshipping anything other than God.

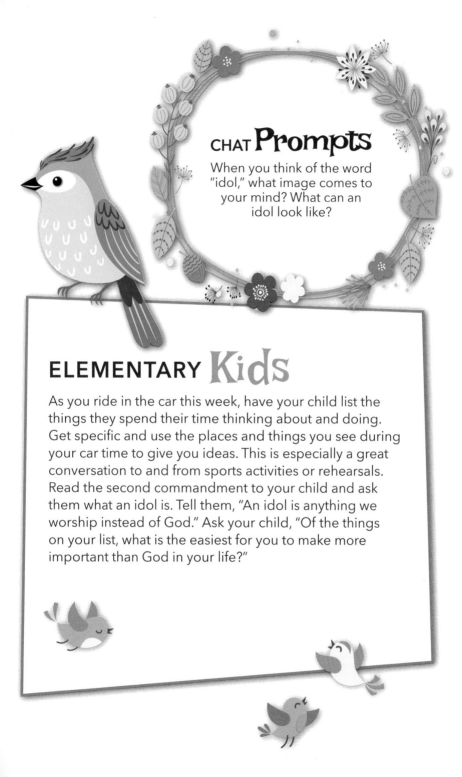

## CHAT **Prompts**

When you think of the word "idol," what image comes to your mind? What can an idol look like?

## ELEMENTARY Kids

As you ride in the car this week, have your child list the things they spend their time thinking about and doing. Get specific and use the places and things you see during your car time to give you ideas. This is especially a great conversation to and from sports activities or rehearsals. Read the second commandment to your child and ask them what an idol is. Tell them, "An idol is anything we worship instead of God." Ask your child, "Of the things on your list, what is the easiest for you to make more important than God in your life?"

# CHAPTER 16

# Don't Use God's Name in Vain

 **MEDITATE**

*You shall not misuse the name of the Lord you God, for the Lord will not hold anyone guiltless who misuses his name.* – Exodus 20:7

Extended passage: Isaiah 9:6-7

 **ANTICIPATE**

● What names have people used to build you up? What names have people used to tear you down?

_____

_____


● Which of God's names are especially meaningful to you? How do they help you relate to God?

_____

_____

# RELATE

"So-FI-ah!"

"Is-a-BEL!"

I could hear the conversation going on upstairs, and I knew by their enunciation that it wasn't a pleasant one. When my girls get angry, suddenly their words are marked by extra syllables, some of which are said with great emphasis.

## NAMES IDENTIFY US

I chose each of my childrens' names with care. I loved each child deeply, even before I held them in my arms, and I wanted their names to speak to the identity and future that I prayed over them. No matter what I once intended when I chose their names, somehow in the heat of the moment, their names are used to inflict pain. And it always strikes them - I can see it in their eyes. Names are personal, and how we use them matters.

## WE CAN RELATE

The third commandment teaches us that God cares deeply about how we use his name. It would be easy for me to share a "thou shalt not" list of taking God's name in vain, but let's consider how living by the third commandment was intended to strengthen our relationship with God and others. How can we not just avoid the misuse of God's name, but take it a step further and use God's name as it was intended? I think it starts by valuing God's name. As we read it and speak it, we can pause to honor the name of God. God's name is power and it identifies the One whose image we bear. Make a commitment to not just avoid misusing God's name, but to use his name to better understand and relate to him, and to teach your child to do the same.

**BEDTIME** While "God" is typically the name we use, the first section of this book outlines some of the other names God uses to identify himself. Consider using some of these names as you talk to God, or as you talk about him with your child. Pause and think about how God identifies himself by using these names. Contemplate how these names help you relate to God, and how he used them to connect with his children – and how he continues to connect with you and your child today.

## PRESCHOOL Kids

Ask your child who we talk to when we pray – what is his name? Share that in the Bible, God has many names, sort of like we have different names and nicknames. Choose one name to introduce to your child, briefly explaining it's meaning. Use this name when you pray with your child before bed. Continue throughout the week, teaching and using a different name each night.

## FAMILY Fun

Read Isaiah 9:6-7 together and share that long before Jesus was born, Isaiah prophesied that these names would be given to Jesus, to describe who he was and what he would do. Write each of these names on a piece of paper and draw or paint what you picture when you hear those names.

## CHAT **Prompts**

What are some of your names, nicknames, or titles? Which are your favorites? What names have you been called that have bothered or hurt you?

## ELEMENTARY Kids

Ask your child if they know some of God's names. If they are confused, explain that God and his people have used different names to describe him - sort of like we have different names, titles - and nicknames. Choose one of God's names and introduce it to your child. Ask what they think the name means, and what it tells them about God. Share that learning God's names helps us know and relate to him better. Use this name as you pray together before bed, and continue with a new name each night this week.

# CHAPTER 17

# Remember the Sabbath and Keep It Holy

 **MEDITATE**

*Remember the Sabbath day by keeping it holy. Six days you shall labor and do all your work, but the seventh day is a sabbath to the Lord your God. On it you shall not do any work, neither you, nor your son or daughter, nor your male or female servant, nor your animals, nor any foreigner residing in your towns. For in six days, the Lord made the heavens and the earth, the sea, and all that is in them, but he rested on the seventh day. Therefore the Lord blessed the Sabbath day and made it holy.* – Exodus 20:8-11

Extended passage: Philemon 1:1-25

 **ANTICIPATE**

● In 5 words or less, describe your family schedule.

_____

_____

● Do you take a full, 24-hour day off from working every week? Why or why not?

_____

_____

## RELATE

I made a promise when I became a dad. I was going to protect my family's schedule. Our time as a family is a precious, perishable commodity. We never get a refund on our time. And while our family said "no" to many things, we still found our calendar filled with activities and our weekends jam-packed with birthday parties, get-togethers, rehearsals, games, and chores. I could barely keep up around the house. I knew things were bad when a friend came over and told me I had six lightbulbs out. It had been so long since they burned out, I didn't even notice them anymore. I was living in a cave.

## NO SABBATH FOR YOU

Honest confession. I was not following the command given by God to "remember the Sabbath and keep it holy." A Sabbath is a God-created, 24-hour period of rest. Sabbath is based on the story of creation in Genesis where God, after working six days creating the universe and everything in it, he rests on the seventh day. I had every excuse to disobey God on this one. My family had things to do, people to see, and projects to complete. "Sorry God. No Sabbath for you." Sadly, I was living in a spiritual cave.

## A RHYTHM OF CONNECTION

I have often skipped over the short letter Paul wrote to a man named Philemon. But this 25 verse letter emphasizes Paul's love for God and others. He uses words like:

"I always thank my God…"
"Your love has given me great joy…"
"I appeal to you on the basis of love…"
"I am sending him – who is my very heart – back to you…"

Paul stopped long enough to remember how much God loved him, Philemon, and the church that met in Philemon's home. I know Paul was in prison at the time, but even so, the rhythm of Paul's life was not bound by the rules of Rome but by meeting with God. You and I could cultivate this same heart by stepping away from the rhythm of work and crazy-busy family life and taking a day to meet with God.

# ON THE ROAD

**AT HOME** When you take a 24-hour period of rest every week, you are telling God 'I trust you with my work, with my home, with my life.'" God is working, even when we are not and when we Sabbath and truly rest we are trusting God implicitly to do his thing. This week, live this truth with your family and commit to a 24 hour period of rest.

## PRESCHOOL Kids

Throughout the week, prepare your preschooler for your Sabbath. Ask them to think of the different things you do on a regular day of the week (grocery shopping, chores, errands, preschool, etc…). Talk about what a Sabbath means. Let them know your family will be taking an entire day to obey God's command to rest and use the time to connect with each other and God.

### FAMILY Fun

This week, do household chores ahead of time. Involve your kids and make sure you get laundry, cleaning, and other items off your checklist so you can rest. Emphasize just how important it is to work hard so you can take a Sabbath as a family!

## CHAT Prompts

Talk with your kids about the things you like to do to recharge as a parent and how those things impact your heart. Maybe you enjoy running or gardening or building stuff. Invite them to join you in those activities on your Sabbath.

## ELEMENTARY Kids

Pace your week at home so you can enjoy a 24-hour period of rest together as a family. Talk about the things your child enjoys experiencing and doing that give them energy and recharge their batteries. Resist the urge to work, check email, even social media. Just rest together and draw close to God.

# CHAPTER 18

# Honor Your Father and Mother

## MEDITATE

*Honor your father and your mother. Then you will live a long time in the land the Lord your God is giving you.* – Exodus 20:12

Extended passage: Ephesians 6:1-4

## ANTICIPATE

● Do you feel like your child honors you?

_____

_____

● What steps have you taken to train your child to honor you?

_____

_____

## RELATE

It had been a long day filled with tantrums and time-outs. Isabel and Sofi were preschoolers, and I was struggling to get them to follow my directions. I remember asking Matt why they listened so much better to him than to me and he said, "Because my words mean something."

## THE PAINFUL TRUTH

His words stung, the connotation being that my words did not mean something. I was angry, but as I stepped back and honestly evaluated myself, I recognized that I was prone to warnings and threats, while I was inconsistent with following through. I would nag and remind instead of enforcing my directions. My desire to have a close relationship with my girls had evolved into a practice of showing leniency and calling it "grace" or a "second chance." God placed such a high value on children learning to honor their parents that he listed it in the ten commandments. And like all of God's commands, we know and trust that it is given for our benefit. God has commanded our children to honor us, but it is our responsibility as parents to train them to obey God. Thankfully he set the perfect example as our Heavenly Father, who guides us along the right path with a balance of love and discipline.

## THE BEST PATH

I'm still a work in progress, and as my children have grown, they've learned new tricks for wearing me down (So. Much. Talking). But I've become better at stating my expectations and following through with consequences, so my children know that my words mean something. The surprising result is that I have a much better relationship with my children when I set the bar high – our home is much more peaceful and harmonious when I train my them to honor me as their mom. God's commands are given to us so that we stay on the best path, the path God intended for us. As parents, we will only strengthen our home and the relationships within our home when we train our children to obey God by honoring us. The words we say need to mean something, so our children grow to not only respect our words but their Heavenly Father's Word as well.

# ON THE ROAD

**WAKE UP** Take some time to evaluate how you are teaching your children to follow God's command. Are you setting clear and age-appropriate expectations then following through? Are you balancing discipline with love, pouring time and affection into your children so that they respond with honor instead of fear?

## PRESCHOOL Kids

Begin your day by reading Exodus 20:12. Explain that God says your child's job is to obey you, and your job is to teach them to follow you – and when they don't obey, your job is to teach them by giving them a consequence (share a few examples of consequences used in your home). Then play a game to practice! Give your child simple directions like jump up and down, and praise them for obeying. Remind them throughout the day that when you give directions, their job is to obey. When you give a consequence, tell them that you are teaching them to obey. Hug and praise them when they make the right choice and follow you. Remind them each day when you wake them up: "God's mercies are new every morning! Today we get a new chance to practice obeying!"

## FAMILY Fun

Work together to show honor to your (Mom's or Dad's) parents. Take time to call or visit to show honor to your parents and your child's grandparents. If that isn't an option, choose another older person to show honor to, perhaps another family member or someone at church.

## CHAT **Prompts**

What makes it difficult for you to obey? Why do you think God commanded us to honor our parents? What are some other ways we can show honor to our parents besides just obeying them?

## ELEMENTARY Kids

Begin your day by reading Exodus 20:12. Grab some coloring supplies and have your child write or sketch what it looks like to "honor" your parents. Explain that God has given you the job of teaching your child to honor you. "Practice" by running through some directions you often give in your home, asking your child how they should respond (feel free to reference their artwork!). Let your child know that you will be obeying God this week by giving directions and following through, expecting your child to obey (praise them when they do!) and giving consequences when they don't. Every day at breakfast, remind your child that "God's mercies are new every morning," and that today you both get a fresh start, a chance to obey God by giving and following directions.

# CHAPTER 19

# You Shall Not Murder

**MEDITATE**

*You shall not murder.* – Exodus 20:13

Extended passage: Matthew 5:17-26

**ANTICIPATE**

● What triggers your anger?

_____

_____


● Describe a time when you acted in anger and regretted it later.

_____

_____

## RELATE

I glanced out the patio door and saw the scene unfold – Isabel was drawing with chalk that she had probably snatched from her sister and Sofi stood over her, metal t-ball bat raised, about to take a swing. At her sister's head. I yelled "STOP!!!" startling Sofi enough to drop the bat before she made contact. She was only four years old, and while she understood that hitting was wrong, she had no idea what the consequences of her action could have been. As I explained how badly Isabel could have been hurt, her eyes welled with tears, and she was as repentant for her actions as she was thankful for my intervention. While the girls often fight, they love each other deeply. But anger sometimes propels them into actions that have unintended consequences.

## GETTING ANGRY

I have a tendency to "skip over" some of the 10 Commandments as if they don't apply to me. Or maybe as if they are rules I've already mastered – "check, I've got that one covered!" But then when I read Jesus's words in Matthew 5, I'm back on the hook. Verse 21 reiterates the commandment not to murder, but then Jesus goes on to say in verse 22, "But I tell you that anyone who is angry with his brother will be subject to judgment…" My legalistic bent wallows in the guilt of this – I struggle with anger towards a handful of people at any given moment. Most of them being my children.

## THE WAY OF RECONCILIATION

This isn't about following the letter of the law. It's never God's heart – to catch his people in sin so he can string them up for it. He longs to turn our hearts toward him, and hearts seething with anger are never turned towards the God Who Is Love. Like a preschooler wielding a metal bat, my anger causes me to speak and act rashly. God warns and intervenes for my protection and others'. If you've sidestepped God's intervention and acted in anger towards someone, keep reading Matthew 5. This God of love doesn't give up on us. Even when we've acted in anger, he paves the way for reconciliation.

# ON THE ROAD

**AT HOME**  Once we've discovered God's commands, we begin the hard work of learning to follow them, but we know that we will sometimes fail. God knew this, too, and always helps us correct our course. If your home is like ours, there is plenty of failure in the anger department. When you or your child act in anger, get back on course by following Jesus's directions to reconciliation.

## PRESCHOOL Kids

When conflict arises, teach your child to reconcile or make peace. When you've been angry (even if your anger was justified), model reconciliation – make peace with your child, especially if you needed to discipline them. Let them know that you love them, give them a hug, and if you acted out in anger than ask for forgiveness.  If your child is the one that's angry, perhaps with another sibling, ask, "how can you make this better?" If they need help, offer suggestions like "give a hug" or "share a toy," and encourage them to focus on restoring the relationship rather than assigning blame.

### FAMILY Fun

Practice some anger management strategies with your family. Brainstorm together or search the internet; try to find strategies that focus on each of the five senses. Remind each other to practice the strategies you've learned when you're feeling angry.

## CHAT **Prompts**

What makes you angry? How does your anger hurt you? How can it hurt your relationships?

# ELEMENTARY Kids

Older children can start initiating reconciliation on their own. Read what Jesus says about anger in Matthew 5 and discuss it with your child – when they aren't angry. Continue modeling reconciliation, making peace with your child after you've been angry. When you notice your child is angry, ask them "How can you make this better? What can you do to restore this relationship."

Family Fun continued: Host a Family Anger Management Night – have fun and practice different strategies, offer prizes for the funniest participant, calmest participant, etc. and hand out diplomas to the "graduates" at the end of the evening.

**CHAPTER 20**

# You Shall Not Commit Adultery

 **MEDITATE**

*You shall not commit adultery.* – Exodus 20:14

Extended passage: Psalm 24:1-10

 **ANTICIPATE**

● What is your favorite article of clothing?

_____

_____

● What does our heart have to do with our actions?

_____

_____

# RELATE

In our hometown, there is a small hipster shop called the Rockford Art Deli where they design and sell shirts and gear with the numbers 815. These three numbers probably do not mean anything to you but for those like me who grew up in Rockford, Illinois they know that 815 is the city's area code. One Christmas, my daughters, received 815 sweatshirts. They wore these comfy shirts with pride and Sofia loved her sweatshirt more than any other article of clothing in her wardrobe. I noticed she was wearing it nearly every day and at first, I was proud, because I bought her the gift. But after a few days, the 815 was starting to show signs of being dirty. I noticed when I sat next to her that her sweatshirt smelled. The smell of the shirt was so bad I struggled to be around her! I finally snuck the prized gift out of her room and threw it in the washing machine.

## MATTERS OF OUR HEART

This week our devotional covers the command not to commit adultery. And as we dig into this commandment, I know your child is not married. Adultery is probably not going to be an issue for your preschooler. We cannot shy away from tough topics like this. In the preceding commandments, we heard God say to his people, "Don't let your heart turn from me and go after other things. Not other gods. Not idols. Hold my name high. Rest in me." God gave his people the law and the ten commandments because he was deeply concerned about their heart. The decisions we make flow out of the river of our heart. The command to not commit adultery is, at its root, about cultivating a pure heart.

## CLEAN HANDS

In Psalm 24, David writes "Who shall ascend the hill of the Lord? And who shall stand in his holy place? He who has clean hands and a pure heart, who does not lift up his soul to what is false, and does not swear deceitfully." God's desire is for you and me to remain clean. To not allow the dirt and grime of sin to cover us with its stink. And the unfathomable truth here is God made our cleansing possible through the sacrifice of Jesus who walked up the hill of Golgatha with a cross on his back to die in our place for the forgiveness of our sins.

# ON THE ROAD

**BED TIME** Moms and dads, help your children keep their heart pure. Consider the influences of culture on their heart. Is what you watch, listen to, read, or play guiding them towards Jesus? What do your child's attitudes and actions speak about the condition of their heart? This week, take the time to commit your hearts to God. Pray a prayer of repentance and dedication with your child as you prepare them for bed. Attitudes and actions speak about the condition of their heart. This week, take the time to commit your hearts to God. Pray a prayer of repentance and dedication with your child as you prepare them for bed.

## PRESCHOOL Kids

Say this prayer one phrase at a time and encourage your child to repeat your words. "Dear God, I ask you to forgive me for the wrong choices I made today. You want my heart to be entirely clean. Please wash away the dirt of my sin and make me clean again. I want to follow you every moment of my life. In Jesus's name, amen.

## FAMILY Fun

Take time to hand wash the dishes together as a family. Highlight how dirty the dishes are before you begin and make sure to point out how clean they are in the end. Reinforce God's desire for our actions and choices to be clean and our hearts pure.

## CHAT **Prompts**

What do you feel when you make a choice you know is wrong? What happens to your heart?

# ELEMENTARY **Kids**

Ask your child to take a moment to think about the choices they made today. Say this prayer one phrase at a time and encourage your child to repeat your words. "Dear God, you know the choices I made today. Some were amazing, and some were not so great. I'm sorry for sinning, and I need you to forgive me. Make me clean again so I can follow you with my whole heart. In Jesus's name, amen.

**CHAPTER 21**

# You Shall Not Steal

 **MEDITATE**

*You shall not steal.* – Exodus 20:15

Extended passage: Ephesians 4:17-32

 **ANTICIPATE**

● How did you spend summer afternoons as a child?

_____

_____

● Did you ever do something wrong and not get caught as a child? What did you "get away with"?

_____

_____

One of my favorite things to do as a kid was walking to the store (less than a mile from my front door) and playing the Street Fighter II arcade game in the store's entrance. My older brother John and I would spend many summer afternoons stopping inside the store to buy a candy bar, camping out by the arcade game, throwing our quarters into the machine and talking trash to each other as we sparred round after round. But over time I realized the more quarters I spent on the candy bars, the fewer quarters I had to learn the finer points of fighting with the world warriors, Blanka and Zangief. So I began to steal the candy bars. Then it became so easy to steal candy bars; I started to take other things too. Candy, hats, cassette tapes, and CDs of Hootie and the Blowfish or the Rocky IV soundtrack joined my stolen collection.

## NEVER CAUGHT

There's a good chance my mom is reading this. I know mom, I was the hard child. The euphoria of getting away with the stealing outweighed the possible consequences. Looking back, I wish someone had caught me.

## FROM STEALING TO GIVING

One of the Ten Commandments has to do with stealing. Sadly, I broke this commandment many times. But the truth is as an adult; the temptation to apply a five finger discount to a Butterfinger is not an issue for me. And it's likely it is not a problem for you. But this command has more to it. God calls his people to do hard things – to live where our earthly pleasure is not our highest goal, where our satisfaction is found in Christ. As his kids, we are called to treasure honesty and hard work. To honor others by valuing what they have and by giving them what we have made. Ephesians 4:28 offers a new interpretation of this commandment when Paul instructs, "Anyone who has been stealing must steal no longer, but must work, doing something useful with their hands, that they may have something to share with those in need." This is part of a longer section of instructions for how the Ephesian church should live.

# ON THE ROAD

**AT HOME** When it comes to obeying the commands of God, sometimes we simply need to redirect our efforts from what is easy to what is hard. It is easy to take something that is not yours. The real work is to train our hands to serve God and others in useful ways generously. Spend your time this week focusing on what it means to obey God in this way.

## PRESCHOOL Kids

Play an opposites game with your preschooler (this will work best with a four-or five-year-old child). What is the opposite of up? Short? Big? Then, talk about this commandment. Say, "One of God's commands is: do not steal. What does it mean to steal something?" Stealing is when we take something that does not belong to us. Then ask your child, "What is the opposite of stealing – taking something away from someone?" Giving! Think of some ways you can give to others this week.

## FAMILY Fun

Make a meal for another family together! Plan the meal, purchase the ingredients, cook and deliver it together. As you work together, remind your family of the ways you are using your hands to give instead of take.

## CHAT **Prompts**

Talk about what your child would like to do as an adult. What skills are required for their dream job? What does that person need to be able to do? Talk about how having that job can be done to help others.

# ELEMENTARY Kids

Have a conversation with your child about stealing. Ask, "Have you ever taken anything that did not belong to you? Tell me what happened." Read Ephesians 4:28 together. Ask, "How can we train our hands to do something useful?" Find a "useful" thing to do together like making cards, drawing pictures, or writing encouraging notes to friends or family members.

# CHAPTER 22

# Do Not Give False Witness Against Your Neighbor

*Do not give false witness against your neighbor.* – Exodus 20:16

Extended passage: James 1:19-27

- Describe a time that you were affected by a rumor that was a lie spread about you, or you were a part of spreading the rumor.

_____

_____

- What helps you remember to "think before you speak"?

_____

_____

Sofi came home from school, and I could tell by the look on her face, it had been a tough day. I asked her about it, and she cast a sideways glance at Isabel (who shrugged), and then Sofi muttered something about it not being a big deal. After some uncomfortable silence on their part and ultimatums on mine, I discovered that a squabble inside the house carried on once they left, and Isabel had gathered a group of sympathizers and shared how cruel her sister "really" was. She hadn't necessarily lied, but without context and to a group of gossip-hungry girls, she had certainly cherry-picked her truths and strung them together without context, and now this group of girls was steering clear of Sofi because she was a menace to society.

## WIDESPREAD DAMAGE

By this time Isabel felt terrible about her mistake. We led her to realize that once you share a hurtful story, you can't take those words back. They will color the hearer's perception of reality forever. We told Isabel that she would have to go back to her friends and tell them the truth, about Sofi, and about herself. Facing the music was a painful lesson for Isabel. A lot of damage is done when you spread rumors, and the damage can't be undone with a simple apology.

## LONG ROAD BACK

This is why the command not to bear false witness against your neighbor shows up in God's Top Ten. Whether it's a bold-faced lie or a subtle twisting of the truth, spreading an untrue or not-quite-true rumor about someone else causes pain and destruction. It damages relationships and reputations, and even if forgiveness is offered, restoration can be a long and challenging journey. When our children speak quickly and hurt others in the process, it's important to pause and help them understand the damage they've caused, and take responsibility to make repairs. It was incredibly difficult for Isabel to take responsibility and have a hard conversation with her friends the next day, but I think that was what stuck with her most, and what will hopefully serve as a reminder to choose her words more carefully in the future.

In a culture where words have far-reaching capabilities thanks to social media and smart phones, a word spoken (or typed) in haste and anger can spread quickly and cause damage beyond our control. This week, have some fun with words and teach your kids to practice pause before they speak.

## PRESCHOOL Kids

Tell your child that you're going to play a game. You'll say a word; then they have to say the first word that they think of quickly, then you'll respond to their word, and so on. When you're finished compare your first and last word – are they very much alike? Share that words can be a lot of fun, and when you were playing your game, it was fun to say words quickly without thinking. But sometimes we say mean words without thinking, and those mean words can hurt people. When we feel angry, it's important to take a break and think before we speak, so our words aren't mean and hurtful.

## FAMILY Fun

Play a game of telephone. Gather your family in a circle and have one person whisper a phrase to the next person. Continue whispering the words around the circle until you reach the last person. Have them say the phrase aloud and see how it compares to the original. Discuss how spreading a rumor can be like playing a game of telephone.

## CHAT **Prompts**

When you've broken God's command and said something unkind and untrue about someone else, what steps should you take to make things right?

# ELEMENTARY Kids

Invite your child to play a game. You'll say a word, then they will say the first word that pops into their mind, then the next person responds with the first word that pops into their mind, and so on. When you're finished, stop and compare your first and last word. Are they similar? How did your words change so quickly? Ask your child if anyone has ever said hurtful words about them. Have they ever said hurtful words without thinking? Read God's command in Exodus 20:16 and discuss how ignoring God's command could hurt others and even ourselves.

**CHAPTER 23**

# You Shall Not Covet

**MEDITATE**

*Do not long for anything that belongs to your neighbor. Do not long for your neighbor's house, wife, male or female servant, ox or donkey.*
– Exodus 20:17

**ANTICIPATE**

- Think of a time you felt you didn't get what you deserved. How did you respond? How did you move on?

_____

_____

- How do you react when your child is ungrateful?
  What is especially frustrating about their ingratitude?

_____

_____

# RELATE

Isabel and Sofi were toddlers when we bought a brand new duplex in a great neighborhood with excellent schools. We considered it a "starter" home when we bought it and planned to sell it and move into a single family home before Isabel started kindergarten. Then the market crashed, and our plans to move were put on hold. I became more and more dissatisfied with our home and found myself longing for a bigger, better home. I struggled to enjoy community groups or play dates hosted by friends with larger homes, taunted by their basements and two-car garages and storage space that went on for days. This longing for what others had made me resentful, ungrateful, and if I'm honest, lonely. We rarely extend invites to our pity-parties.

## START OVER

God doesn't explain why coveting is a sin, but I have a hunch that when he issues that commandment, he had our best interests in mind. When we feel that we don't have what we deserve, we see God as the withholder of what we want, rather than the giver of all good things. This sin of coveting, longing for what we don't have, goes all the way back to the Garden. It's a response to the lie that God doesn't love us, that he chooses not to give us the thing that would bring us happiness.

## TREASURING THE GIFT

As parents, we are quick to point out our child's ungratefulness. When they complain that they got the smaller piece, or less attention, or fewer things, we often feel exasperated. And yet we don't ever really outgrow this "not fair" attitude. We carry this attitude until it becomes adult-sized, and we covet the bigger house, the more attentive spouse, the better vacation, the thinner thighs, the more cushioned bank account, the less-painful relationship and the list goes on. Sometimes we covet out of valid desires, we long for things that would lesson great hardship, but this longing never fills the emptiness. The only antidote is Jesus, who has set in our hearts a longing for eternity with him, a longing that he has already promised to fulfill.

**WAKE UP**  We often start our day counting our losses (we didn't get enough sleep, we don't have enough time) and end our day doing the same (I didn't finish this, I failed that). This practice only contributes to a longing for what we lack, and what we perceive someone else has. Focus instead on your blessings. Make it a habit of waking up and falling asleep counting the gifts your Father has given you. When your heart still struggles with longing, anchor your hope in Christ who has promised to fulfill our deepest longings for Eternity.

## PRESCHOOL Kids

When you go to wake up your child, have them count three blessings – people or things that give them joy. When you put them to bed, do the same. Pray and thank God for loving us and blessing us with good things. When your child grumbles and complains about what someone else has, respond with: I know it's hard when you feel like you don't have what you want, but it helps to remember our blessings. And remember that God has promised that someday we will be with him and we will have more than what we could ever imagine.

## FAMILY Fun

Gather some of your gently used and no longer needed items and donate them to a local charity. Take inventory of your overflowing blessings, and thank God for blessing you so much that you can be a blessing to others.

## CHAT **Prompts**

Have you ever been jealous of something that someone else had? How did that make you feel? How did your jealousy affect that relationship?

# ELEMENTARY Kids

Tell your child that together you're going to practice a new habit. Every morning when you wake up, and every evening when you go to bed, you're going to count your blessings, naming the things and people that God has given you and that bring you joy. Remind your child to count their blessings when you wake them up and put them to bed. Take a moment to pray and thank God together. When you notice your child wanting what someone else has, remind them of their blessings. Let them know that our hearts will always feel longing because we are created to be with God, and until we are with him in Heaven, something will always be missing. Remind them of his promise to fulfill this longing.

# CHAPTER 24

# Love God

*Love the Lord your God with all your heart and with all your soul and with all your strength.* – Deuteronomy 6:5

Extended passage: Deuteronomy 6:1-9

● Name three things you love.

_____

_____

● What does the bedtime routine look like in your house?

_____

_____

## RELATE

Our family has established a bedtime routine for our son Zion. Nearly every night through his four-year lifespan we follow the same steps. We give Z a bath, put on his PJs, set him up with his best friend George (a gray stuffed dog), and we sing him a song my wife wrote.

Zion, little Zion, little Zion it's okay
It's not worth the crying little Zion it's okay
It's time for you to go to sleep so close your eyes and start to dream
Zion, little Zion, little Zion it's okay

Once Zion became a preschooler, I added a final piece to the routine. I kiss him goodnight, say "I love you," walk to his door and ask, "Who loves you?" Zion always responds, "Daddy." And before I close the door I tell him, "That's right, buddy."

## HOW WE LOVE

Love is one of the driving forces of parenting. We love our children, and we teach them to love others. God's story makes it clear: we were designed to love. And we read a command concerning love in the book of Deuteronomy, which was a book laying out God's laws for his people. God commanded Israel, "Love the Lord your God with all your heart and with all your soul and with all your strength." This command is simple – we must give our love to the one who deserves it most. Every part of our being must radiate vibrant, effervescent love for our God.

## OUR HIGHEST GOAL

Of all the things we will teach our children to love – our favorite sports teams, a movie series, various family traditions, vacation spots, or foods – the greatest is to love God with everything they have. To love with your entire heart, soul, and mind is to display love through everything we do and everything we are. Our thoughts, actions, words, work, play, even our understanding of the world around us – all of this must be saturated in love for God.

# ON THE ROAD

**BEDTIME** God's people refer to Deuteronomy 6:4-9 as the "Shema," which means "prayer." The Shema is critical because it contains the most prominent, most fundamental truth about God. Jesus refers to this passage as the greatest commandment in the Old Testament in Matthew 23. What does it look like to love God with everything we have? To leave nothing behind in our commitment and fervor to love God? This week, add a piece to your bedtime routine focusing on loving God.

## PRESCHOOL Kids

Integrate a moment in your bedtime routine for you and your preschooler to express love to God. Say, "God deserves our love. Let's tell God how much we love him together." Start with the phrase, "God I love you because" and allow your child to finish the sentence. Take turns completing the statement until each of you have shared three things. Help your preschooler come up with ideas if they need help.

### FAMILY Fun

If you've been going through the devotional, you've looked at a lot of different names for God and ways God reveals himself to us. Use what you've learned so far with your child to draw a picture of what you love about God!

## CHAT **Prompts**

What does it look like when someone loves you very much? What do they do? What do they say?

# ELEMENTARY **Kids**

As kids grow older, the bedtime routine can be cut short, or moms and dads no longer are involved. Make sure you spend some dedicated time with your child before they go to sleep. Share some of the things you love about your child. Read Deuteronomy 6:5 together and verbally express to God some of the things you love about him. Prompt your child to join your prayer.

**CHAPTER 25**

# Love Your Neighbor

## MEDITATE

*"...Love your neighbor as yourself..."* – Mark 12:21

Extended passage: Mark 12:28-34

## ANTICIPATE

● What does it look like to love your neighbor as yourself?

_____

_____


● In what ways do you show love to your neighbor?

_____

_____

## RELATE

Our three-year-old son Zion loves our neighbors. Sometimes he plays with them for hours, following their eight-year-old little boy around like a loyal puppy. I love the way this kid plays with and cares for my son – teaching him to shoot hoops, pushing him on the swings, waiting for him to catch up when playing tag. In his own way, he is showing Zion how to be a good neighbor.

## GOOD NEIGHBORS

Sometimes loving your neighbor is easy. And sometimes it's not. As a host home for Safe Families, we often open our home to children whose families are in crisis. This fall, Isabel and Sofi, who are ten and eleven, shared their bedroom and bond with another little girl for over two months. They made great memories, and they also made their share of drama, bickering over clothes or toys or attitudes that flared in close quarters. Sometimes I pulled Isabel and Sofi aside to talk about the hard parts of loving your neighbor – caring for one another, bearing one another's burdens, extending grace and forgiveness when it would be easier to carry a grudge. When a placement ends, and we send a child back to their home, we reflect on our time together. We always come to the conclusion that we are better for having them with us. That by loving our neighbor in this way, we learn more about God and how he loves us.

## LOOKING OUT FOR OTHERS

Most of us are prone to look out for ourselves first, and then look out for others when it doesn't carry too much risk or inconvenience or cost. But Jesus didn't place any qualifiers or stipulations when he commanded us to love our neighbor. In fact, his only clarification was to love them "as yourself." This type of love looks out for the well-being of others as naturally as we look out for our own. Sometimes this comes as easily as shooting hoops with the kid next door, and sometimes it's as bumpy and messy as sheltering a child who carries more brokenness than belongings. As children loved by God, we are called and even blessed to share his love with our neighbor.

# ON THE ROAD

**ON THE ROAD** While Jesus wasn't commanding us only to love our literal neighbors, showing love to the people in our neighborhood is a great place to start. Commit as a family to showing God's love to your neighbors this week. If you don't have neighbors, get creative – share God's love with neighbors at a local park, fire or police station, nursing home, or anywhere you feel prompted to love your neighbor.

## PRESCHOOL Kids

Read Mark 12:21 to your preschooler. Ask them if they know what a neighbor is, then see if they can name or describe any of your neighbors. Then take a walk as a family, greeting any neighbors you pass along the way. Take your time, stopping to say hello, or asking about their day. When you get home, pray for the neighbors you met on the road.

## FAMILY Fun

Choose a neighbor – someone in you or your child's circle of friends, classmates, co-workers, or family members – that could use some love and encouragement. Make a card, bake cookies, or choose another tangible way to show love to this person. Then commit to praying for them and loving them as yourself.

## CHAT **Prompts**

Who are the neighbors we live by? Who does the Bible say is your neighbor? How can YOU love your neighbor as yourself today?

## ELEMENTARY Kids

Read Mark 12:21 together and ask your child to explain the verse in their own words. See how many neighbors you can name or describe together. Then take a family walk around your neighborhood, greeting neighbors along the way. Encourage your child to show love to your neighbors by sharing a smile or a simple hello. Model love as you greet your neighbors, asking how they are doing or introducing yourself if you haven't met. Pray together once you get home, thanking God for your neighbors and asking him to help you love your neighbor as yourself.

# CHAPTER 26

# Tithe

Bring the whole tithe into the storehouse, that there may be food in my house. Test me in this," says the Lord Almighty, "and see if I will not throw open the floodgates of heaven and pour out so much blessing that there will not be room enough to store it.    – Malachi 3:10

Extended passage: Malachi 3:6-12

● What are the top five things you spend money on each month?

_____

_____

● How do conversations about money make you feel?

_____

_____

## RELATE

I'm the dad who gets a little hardcore about money. As four-and five-year-olds, my kids would pass a fountain filled with coins and ask me for loose change. My response was the same every time. "I worked way too hard for this money to throw it in a bucket of water." My wife reminded me often that I would need a bucket for all the tears my children were weeping due to my response. But the money wasting fountain was not my only issue.

## TOOTH FAIRY

I completely ignored the tooth fairy with my kids out of a deeply held conviction that the tooth fairy is the worst scam possible for everyone involved. First off, teeth are just disgusting, and as a dad, I'm often the one having to go after these tiny bones inside the mouths of my children. I am getting the complete raw end of the tooth fairy deal. Second, the whole exchange of teeth for money makes no sense at all. I worked too hard for the money we have to make my kids think someone magically broke into their room to pay them for their nasty teeth. No way. My wife reminded me that I would probably need to save the money I would have given them for their teeth to establish a therapy fund.

## FROM GETTING TO GIVING

Money is a topic the Bible extensively addresses because it is so deeply anchored in our hearts. And one of God's commands related to money is to give back a portion of what we have to God. This is called a "tithe." Moms and dads, here's where we can get way off the rails when it comes to finances. We think we earned everything we have, so we hold onto it as tightly as possible. God commands us to give back a portion of what he has provided, knowing that giving is the thing that moves us forward. Take time to consider, are you obeying God in this area of your life? Are you modeling for your children what it means to give back to God a tithe generously?

# ON THE ROAD

**AT HOME** There were many years of my life when money was so tight; I convinced myself that I did not have enough to give God anything. But as I read Malachi 3, I was convicted. God offers a crazy challenge – asking his people to test his generosity through obedience in the area of tithing. I took God up on this challenge, and God has never failed to provide over and above what my family needs.

## PRESCHOOL Kids

Preschoolers can begin to understand the value of money, and you can shape that understanding by allowing them to earn it and put it into categories. Figure out how best to accomplish a regular rhythm for your child to make a set amount of money and use three envelopes or jars to divide it into "Spend," "Save," and "Give." Use the money in the Give jar to give back to God.

## FAMILY Fun

Give your tithe together as a family. Make it a cheerful celebration! Imagine together how God might use your gift to make a difference in other people's lives.

## CHAT Prompts

Has God ever provided for your family when you needed help? Share this story with your family and talk about how this experience made you feel.

# ELEMENTARY Kids

If you have not done so already, create a weekly set of chores for your child to accomplish and set aside an amount of money they can earn from their work. Create three envelopes or containers to divide the money: Spend, Save, and Give. Read Malachi 3:10 and invite them to take the challenge God gives to tithe.

# CHAPTER 27

# Salvation

**MEDITATE**

*For it is by grace you have been saved, through faith—and this is not from yourselves, it is the gift of God— not by works, so that no one can boast.* - Ephesians 2:8-9

Extended passage: Ephesians 2:1-10

**ANTICIPATE**

● Who is your favorite character from a book?

_____

_____

● What is the best story you've ever read to your child?

_____

_____

# RELATE

When my daughters Isabel and Sofia were in preschool, I bought them a children's book which encapsulated the whole narrative of the Bible. Because I wanted Isabel and Sofia to experience the beauty of the language and the amazing illustrations over time, I stretched out the experience of reading the book over several nights. We would read the story together before bedtime. Night time reading had been a longtime tradition, but both of the girls seemed to be particularly interested in finishing this storybook. One night, we were finishing an experiment with apples and lemon juice and the girls were sitting on the floor in our upstairs bathroom. Since bedtime was drawing near, I thought it would be a great time to finish our book.

## PART OF YOUR STORY

I opened it up and read from the time of the 400-year silence through the end where celebration of the new heaven and new earth was revealed.  I got to the final page and read its invitation to take an individual place in God's Story and my daughter Sofia asked excitedly, "How can I do that?" We talked about sins and forgiveness and making Jesus her Savior. Then we gathered together and she prayed by herself, with her eyes shut so tight as she stood on the bathroom stool, "God, I want to be part of your story...."

## THE STORY

As I took a moment to reflect on the experience, I realized that Sofia knew so much about the Bible. She had been in church her entire life. We read God's Word and prayed together; I asked her questions about her experiences in church. There is no doubt that at four years old, Sofia knew the stories of the Bible, but somehow she had missed THE story. And once THE story was told to her in words she could understand, she had to be part of it. There was no choice but to join its sweeping movement, to be completely caught up in it and to find the part God had for her to play. And the heavens rejoiced when her name was penned into the Book of Life

# ON THE ROAD

**AT HOME** For Sofia, there was something about seeing the whole story that unlocked the gift of God in the story. It is abundantly clear God has given each of us the free gift of salvation. And you may be wondering about how you might have a salvation conversation with your children. Don't worry, you can do this!

## PRESCHOOL Kids

This week, find a great storybook Bible and sit down to read it with your children. Take your time and help them see the whole story. Make sure you focus on the death and resurrection of Jesus. As you read those stories, ask your child to think about what Jesus has done so all of the wrong choices they have made could be made right, and completely forgiven.

### FAMILY Fun

Watch a movie or show involving a rescue and talk about how the rescuer saved the person in need.

## CHAT **Prompts**

When your child has made a mistake or wrong choice this week, talk about the results of their decision and how Jesus saves us from our sin.

## ELEMENTARY Kids

With your child, read Ephesians 2:1-9 and think about God's incredible gift of salvation. Ask them, "Have you accepted God's gift of salvation?" If you sense they are ready to make that decision, walk them through the ABC steps. Admit you are a sinner in need of God's grace (Romans 3:23; 6:23). Believe in Jesus (John 3:16). Confess out loud that you put your faith and trust in Jesus (Romans 10:9-10). Now celebrate!

**CHAPTER 28**

# God Gives Us Eternal Life

 MEDITATE

*When you sin, the pay you get is death. But God gives you the gift of eternal life because of what Christ Jesus our Lord has done.*
– Romans 6:23 (NIRV)

Extended passage: Romans 6:15-23

 ANTICIPATE

- When was the last time your family experienced a meltdown en route to the car?

_____

_____

- What comes to mind when you think of eternal life?

_____

_____

## RELATE

It was Good Friday and I was prepping three girls for our church's Good Friday service. Between the hair curling and dresses and accessories, everything went downhill and by the time we were headed out the door for church, they were crying and I was yelling and this Friday felt anything but Good. I sat in the driver's seat wondering what I could do to make things better, because surely showing up to Good Friday service a hot, teary mess of anger and frustration was a case in missing the point. And then I heard a still, small voice... my 7 year old's, actually... "Mommy, can we just start over?"

## START OVER

It sounded like a perfect Good Friday solution. So we talked about our day, confessed our sins, asked for forgiveness from each other and our Savior. I shared with them that when you sin, the payment is death but that Good Friday means that Jesus paid the price of death. And we are offered the gift of eternal life instead. By the end, Isabel was giggling, simply filled with joy, her burden of guilt lifted and replaced with hope instead.

## TREASURING THE GIFT

In this world of immediate feedback and instant gratification, this gift of eternal life feels far off, almost unreal. But in those moments spent reflecting on God's gift, on the power of sin erased and eternal life given in its place, I realized that eternal life is a gift that I experience – in part – here and now. Earlier in this passage, Paul shares that we were once slaves of sin, but now we are free to live this New Life, joined with Christ NOW and for all Eternity. This free-from-sin-and-death life gives me a longing and a hope for the day when I can experience eternal life fully – not only free from sin's consequences, but free from the presence of sin itself. When we take time to experience forgiveness, to reflect on what Jesus did to erase our payment and offer us the gift of eternal life, we experience the joy found in the hope of eternal life.

# ON THE ROAD

If your family is anything like ours, you often experience a breakdown en route to the car. This week, when you and your child find yourself past the breaking point, a hot teary mess buckled into carseats and driver seats, take a deep breath. Start over.

## PRESCHOOL Kids

Give your child a moment to calm down. Talk about their sins or bad choices, as well as your own. Share that God's Word says that the payment for sin is death, but the good news is that Jesus already paid our payment and God wants to give us the gift of eternal life instead! Someday we will live with God forever, where there will be no more bad choices and no more payment or sad things that happen. Take a moment before you head on your way to celebrate God's gift – cheer, clap, sing a song of praise!

## FAMILY Fun

Gather some art supplies (crayons, markers, play dough, paints – whatever you have available) and create a family art project that represents what you think Heaven will look like. If you need help getting started, choose some verses from Revelation 21. Talk about God's amazing promise of eternal life.

## CHAT Prompts

What do you think Eternal Life with Jesus will be like? What do you look forward to? What do you wonder about?

# ELEMENTARY Kids

Let your child know how you feel and share that you both need a moment to calm down. Then ask them what bad choices they made, and what they think the payment or consequence should be. Continue by sharing how you sinned. Read Romans 6:23 and ask your child what they think that means, then explain that verse in your own words. Share how this gift of eternal life affects you personally, how it gives you hope or joy. Then before you head on your way, take a moment to celebrate God's gift of eternal life!

**CHAPTER 29**

# Holy Spirit

## MEDITATE

*If you then, though you are evil, know how to give good gifts to your children, how much more will your Father in heaven give the Holy Spirit to those who ask him!* – Luke 11:13

Extended passage: Luke 11:1-13

## ANTICIPATE

● What did your children ask to receive for their last birthday?

_____

_____

● What did you give your child on their last birthday?

_____

_____

## RELATE

Somehow in today's Pinerest-focused, social-media driven parenting world. A simple birthday party has turned into a crafting project and baking extravaganza to rival the crowning of royalty.
Your kid is turning 5 or 9, take it easy fella.

## GIFTS

Regardless of the size of a birthday party or the level of detail, the birthday gifts play an important role. And there's a big difference between a fun gift and getting something you need. Growing up, I always received gifts from both categories. Two pairs of pants and a football were wrapped under the tree. Socks and a small building bricks set. My kids receive sensible gifts along with toys and games. But if you asked my children or your children or any child in the world, "Would you rather get a button up shirt to wear to church or a light saber?" no one, ever, would go with the Sunday shirt. Why is that?

## WHAT WE WANT

We gravitate towards what we want, not what we need. My children have never asked for socks and shoes for their birthday. They only ask for toys, games, or media. They find catalogs and scroll through Amazon searching for what they want. Walking through the store their favorite activity is finding an item and describing how badly they need it. Despite their best efforts, I've learned to give my kids both what they desire and what is helpful to them. In Luke 11, Jesus uses the metaphor of a father giving gifts to his children to represent God giving us the Holy Spirit.

## HOW MUCH MORE

The Holy Spirit is a gift God our Father loves to give. John uses the words "how much more" to show just how dedicated and motivated God is to answer our requests for the Holy Spirit in our lives. We often come to God out of desperate need, when things may be going poorly or when we are out of answers or hope. What would it look like to come to God out of delight in Him? To ask for the gift of the Holy Spirit out of a desire to see God do new things in your life and the life of your family? He's waiting.

# ON THE ROAD

Instead of focusing on games or books while riding in the car this week, use the time to notice and think through what you and your child desire. Consider the messages you encounter and how they impact what you want.

## PRESCHOOL Kids

One of a preschooler's favorite things to do is talk about the things they want (for their birthday or Christmas). Discuss and list your preschooler's wants. Then take time to talk about the things your preschooler needs. Ask them, "What are the things you need every day?" Remind your child that the Holy Spirit is something we need, but it is also a gift God loves to give.

## FAMILY Fun

Have your children look through their toys and pick out a few things to donate to a family shelter. Help them practice giving. Remind them that the Holy Spirit teaches us to give.

## CHAT Prompts

What do you see as you look out the window when we are driving? Do you want anything you see?

## ELEMENTARY Kids

Ask your child if they remember the list of presents they wanted for their last birthday or last Christmas and have them list the presents they received. Ask them, "What was the number one thing you wanted? Why did you want that so badly?" Read Luke 11:13 with them. Remind them how we can ask God for the gift of the Holy Spirit who is present to guide and help us, no matter what.

**CHAPTER 30**

# Individual Gifts

 **MEDITATE**

*...Each of you has received a gift in order to serve others. You should use it faithfully. If you speak, you should do it like one speaking God's very words. If you serve, you should do it with the strength God provides. Then in all things God will be praised through Jesus Christ.*

– 1 Peter 4:10-11 (NIRV)

Extended passage: 1 Peter 4:1-11

 **ANTICIPATE**

- What are some unique talents or abilities that God has gifted you with, and how do you enjoy using them to serve others?

_____

_____

- Think of one or more unique talents or abilities that God has gifted your child(ren) with.

_____

_____

Most parents enjoy a particular stage in their child's life more than others, and when they are parenting through that stage, they thrive. For me, it's the preschool stage. I am totally winning at parenting when I have a 3-5 year old. Tweens perplex me. Babies turn me into a mombie. But all of my gifts are clearly targeted towards conversing with, teaching, and maneuvering through Target aisles with my preschoolers in tow. The other day I was walking through the store with my three-year old son Zion, and I was literally stopped by Santa, who complimented me on my sweet boy's manners and a job well done as his mom. Thank goodness he wasn't there two days later for a shopping excursion with my tween girls. While I love my kids in and through all the other phases, I often lean into the gifts of other wise parents and grandparents in my life throughout those phases that I am not quite as gifted in.

## UNIQUELY GIFTED

God has gifted each of us uniquely, and what we learn here in 1 Peter, is that those gifts have been given to us so that we can serve others. We haven't been given all the gifts; we are interdependent on one another so that as we each use our gifts, we can glorify God together. Scripture paints a picture of the Church as a body of believers who join together, serving one another, complimenting each others' weaknesses with strengths, using their gifts to glorify God.

## STARTING AT HOME

Using our gifts always involves serving others, and as parents, we are given the unique opportunity to use our gifts to serve our children in our home every single day. Whatever your gifts are, use them first and foremost at home as you serve your family. Recognize your weaknesses and surround yourself with others who are gifted in those areas, so they can compliment you with their strengths. Begin praying about and noticing your child's gifts. Affirm those gifts and give your child opportunities to use their gifts to serve others. As you serve each other as a family, you glorify God together.

# ON THE ROAD

**WAKE UP** Even young children can begin recognizing their gifts and using them to serve others. Begin affirming your child's gifts and make your home a place where everyone uses their gifts to serve one another.

## PRESCHOOL Kids

Begin your day by using your gifts to serve your family. Make a special breakfast, write notes of encouragement, share a hug or a back rub – think of unique ways to model what it looks like to use your gifts to serve others. At breakfast, talk with your preschooler about their gifts. Ask them what they think they are good at, and let them know that God gives each of us gifts so that we can serve or help others. Share how it felt to use your gifts to serve your family that morning and help your preschooler make a plan to use their gifts to serve someone today.

### FAMILY Fun

Play a game of charades together. Brainstorm a list of each other's gifts. Choose one person to act out one of those gifts while the others try to guess what it is and whose gift it is, then switch places.

## CHAT Prompts

Why do you think God gave each of us different gifts? Why is it important to use our gifts to serve others?

# ELEMENTARY Kids

Turn your family's morning routine into an opportunity to serve each other. Identify at least one gift for each family member – is someone quick to offer encouragement? A natural at keeping their room neat and tidy? Encourage each family member to use their gift(s) to serve one another. At breakfast, talk about how each person used their gift, and how it helped the family. Read 1 Peter 4:11 and discuss why God gives us gifts and why he wants us to use them to serve others.

# CHAPTER 31

# The Gift of Life

How great is the love the Father has given us so freely! Now we can be called children of God. And that's what we really are!

– 1 John 3:1a (NIRV)

Extended passage: 1 John 3:1-10

● How would you describe yourself?

_____

_____


● What does it mean to you to know that you are God's child?

_____

_____

## RELATE

The year Sofi was in pre-k, she was very excited to be in "Miss Noel's class" and while I was nervous about balancing my roles as "Mom" and "Teacher," that year was filled with memories I will cherish forever. It turns out that being the Teacher's daughter in preschool is basically like being a celebrity – everyone wanted to be Sofi's friend and everyone thought she was so lucky to have "Miss Noel" as her mom. No joke, parents would tell me that their child would play "school" at home and enlist siblings and stuffed animals to play the parts of Miss Noel and Sofi. While I was intentional in not showing partiality to Sofi while in class, she knew who she was – my daughter – and as such, she knew that she was deeply loved.

## CELEBRATE GOD'S GIFT

John opens this chapter with a celebration of God's gift of love, given freely to us – his children! This gift means that we are deeply and personally loved by someone more renown than a classroom teacher – we are sons and daughters to our Savior, Creator, King! This gift of love identifies us. We aren't simply a face in the crowd, we are dearly loved children. We aren't the sum of our accomplishments or even our mistakes, we are cherished sons and daughters. When we are knee-deep in the ordinary or overwhelming tasks that make up our lives, we are seen and known by a Father who lavishes us with his great love!

## WHAT WE REALLY ARE

In my daily pursuit of what's next, as I'm counting down to deadlines and nap times, and crowding my margins with never-ending tasks, I rarely think of my identity. I lay awake charting my failures, plotting ways to make up where I've fallen short. But what if, instead, I received this gift of God's great love? What if I celebrated my identity as his child. And what if – *what if* – I taught my son and daughters to do the same? So at the end of each day, the only thing that mattered was *"Now we can be called children of God. And that's what we really are!"* Then this gift of love, freely given to me, becomes a fruit produced in my own life and shared with my child.

## ON THE ROAD

**BEFORE BED** Take time to consider what you are teaching your child about their identity. How can you be intentional about letting them know you love them for who they are, and that the most important thing about them is that they are a dearly loved child of God?

## PRESCHOOL Kids

Tuck your preschooler into to bed and tell them, "(Name), you are my child and I love you always." Then let them know that the most important thing about them is that they are God's child. Share what this means to you personally, and then pray 1 John 3:1 over your child as a blessing before saying goodnight.

## FAMILY Fun

Create a piece of art with your name. Have your child write their name on a sheet of paper, or do it for them. Then decorate the paper showing things they love, words that describe them, favorite colors, etc. Write 'Child of God' on the paper and hang up where all can see to remind them of their true identity.

## CHAT **Prompts**

What makes you feel good about yourself? What are some kind things others have said about you? What are some unkind things?

## ELEMENTARY **Kids**

Tuck your child into bed, letting them know that no matter how big they get, they will always be your child. Tell them, "(Name), you are my child and I love you always." Ask them what they think that means – how does it feel to know that you will always love them? Then ask what they think the most important thing about them is. Affirm those things as interesting or important (or if they are negative or untrue things, address those by comparing them to Scripture), and then let your child know that the most important thing about them is that they are God's child. Share what this means to you personally and invite your child to share what it means to them. Then pray 1 John 3:1 over your child as a blessing before saying goodnight.

# CHAPTER 32

# Joy

## MEDITATE

*You make known to me the path of life; you will fill me with joy in your presence, with eternal pleasures at your right hand.*
— Psalm 16:11

Extended passage: Psalm 16:1-11

## ANTICIPATE

● What do you most enjoy doing?

_____

_____

● What is the best trip you've ever been on?

_____

_____

# RELATE

Several years ago, we decided to plan a family vacation to Disney World. To make the trip happen, our family made extreme changes. We saved every penny we could find. We stopped eating out. We clipped coupons. We cut back on date nights, movies, and desserts. When you start cutting out ice cream, you know it's serious.

## GOING ALL OUT

Once enough money was saved, we went all out for the trip. We stayed on Disney property, rented a limo to go from our house to the airport, made reservations to dine with characters, lined up all the rides we wanted to go on, we even met personally with Peter Pan and Wendy. We ate like kings and queens in the castle and we had the best strawberry shortcake in the world (hint: it's at the Hoop-Dee-Doo Revue in Fort Wilderness and I promise, it will change your life).

## BEING TOGETHER

As the trip came to an end, I sat down with my daughter Isabel and asked her, "What did you enjoy most about this vacation?" Isabel answered, "Just being together." Selfishly, I thought to myself, "We could have saved a lot of money and just hung out at home!" But the thought stuck with me. The real magic was not manufactured by Walt Disney, it was the joy of being together. Joy was the real gift.

## REAL JOY

In Psalm 16:11, David writes about joy in the presence of God. For it is with God, David experiences authentic, enduring joy. The pleasure of the kingdom likely abounded for Israel's greatest king, but the real gift was being with God. Sometimes I feel the pressure of going above and beyond to bring my children happiness. But the truth of the matter is they delight in being with me more than they delight in the things I could buy them. It was great to meet the "Fab Five" at Chef Mickey's, but the best part was doing it together. My encouragement to you is delight in the presence of your Heavenly Father. To draw real joy from God-closeness. If you're feeling the pressure to do better or do more as a parent, remember where real joy and fulfillment come from.

# ON THE ROAD

**WAKE UP** Truthfully examine your heart and your home. Consider the places, moments, people, and things you draw joy from. Think about the kind of joy you experience with each of those things. Do you delight, as David writes in Psalm 16, in being in the presence of God? What could this look like in the life of your family?

## PRESCHOOL Kids

Help your preschooler understand what real joy is. Throughout the week, ask them different questions during wake up time like "What do you think will be the best part of your day? What does the best part of your day feel like?" Tell your child, "The good feelings you experience during the best part of your day, that's joy!" Spend time sharing what you take joy in and give examples of when you experience joy as a parent.

### FAMILY Fun
Being joyful often involves laughter. Try to make each other laugh without saying any words!

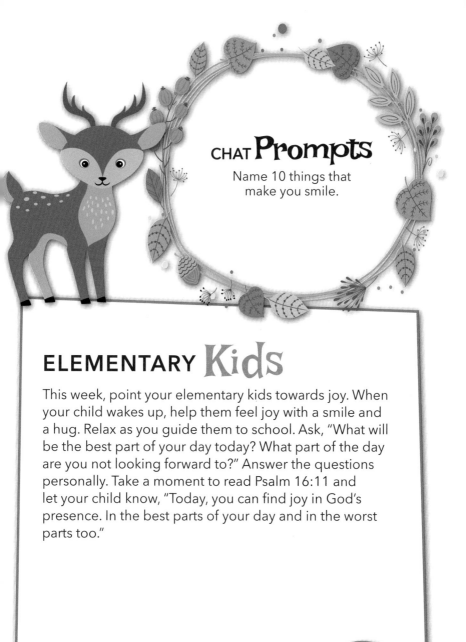

# CHAT Prompts

Name 10 things that make you smile.

# ELEMENTARY Kids

This week, point your elementary kids towards joy. When your child wakes up, help them feel joy with a smile and a hug. Relax as you guide them to school. Ask, "What will be the best part of your day today? What part of the day are you not looking forward to?" Answer the questions personally. Take a moment to read Psalm 16:11 and let your child know, "Today, you can find joy in God's presence. In the best parts of your day and in the worst parts too."

**CHAPTER 33**

# The Gift of Life
## *with Isabel Guevara*

 **MEDITATE**

*"I leave my peace with you. I give my peace to you. I do not give it to you as the world does. Do not let your hearts be troubled. And do not be afraid."* – John 14:27 (NIRV)

Extended passage: John 14:15-31

 **ANTICIPATE**

● What is troubling your heart? What is causing fear in your life?

_____

_____

● How has God's peace given you comfort in a difficult time?

_____

_____

# RELATE

When I was seven, my family and I were told that I would need to have surgery. I had a small lump in my neck and the specialist thought it might be lymphoma. One night, while I was sleeping, I had a dream: a bright light appeared and I knew it was God. He told me to trust in him. A few weeks later, my grandparents were taking my family and I to the American Girl Doll Store. My grandpa accidentally took a wrong turn on the way there. What I saw was amazing: right in front of me was the hospital where I was to have my surgery. In that moment, peace flooded over me and I knew that God was right there with me. God wanted to prove that he was in control and I could trust in him.

## PEACE BRINGS PERSEVERANCE

The words in John 14:27 were spoken by Jesus to his disciples. He knew that he would be leaving them, and they would face difficult times. But he promised them that he would give them peace so they would not need to fear. At the time, the disciples didn't understand what Jesus meant. But as we read the New Testament, we see that Jesus' – promise of peace helped them persevere through persecution – they were not afraid, but instead they openly trusted God. They prayed as they were being stoned, sang while in prison, and shared the gospel when their lives were threatened.

## PEACE IN DIFFICULTY

People often talk about how God is good and that he helps us. But during that time, I felt that if God was truly good, he would heal me so that I didn't need surgery. However, God used my fears and even my surgery to give me peace and show me that I could trust him. This verse doesn't promise that good things will always happen; it tells me that God will always give me peace. This gift of God's peace overcame my fear and gave me great comfort in a difficult time. I have faced hard things in my life, but I always remember how God gave me peace and I have hope because he continues to give me peace in the midst of difficulty.

# ON THE ROAD

Memorize John 14:27 so you can share it with your child on the road. As you drive your child to school, church, or daycare, pray that God will give them the gift of peace while you are away from them. Teach them that God is always with them, and that his gift of peace will help them not to be afraid.

## PRESCHOOL Kids

As you buckle your child into their car seat, ask them how they feel when you are away. What do they worry about? What helps them feel better? As you drive to wherever you will be dropping them off, let them know that God is always with them, and that Jesus promised to give us peace so that we don't have to be afraid. Before you say goodbye, pray together, thanking Jesus for his gift of peace.

## FAMILY Fun

Create a new tradition: whenever you drop your child off, say "God's peace be with you." Write it on the inside window of the car by where they sit with liquid chalk or dry erase markers.

## CHAT Prompts

What makes you feel afraid?
What does peace feel like?

# ELEMENTARY Kids

As you are driving, ask your child how you can be praying for them while you are away. What troubles or concerns do they have? What helps them feel comforted? Remind them that God is always with them. Practice saying John 14:27 and invite your child to learn the verse as well. Ask them what Jesus meant when he promised to give us peace. How can that give them comfort when you are away? Together, thank Jesus for his gift of peace

**CHAPTER 34**

# Patience

*But if we hope for what we do not yet have, we wait for it patiently. In the same way, the Spirit helps us in our weakness.* – Romans 8:25-26a

Extended passage: Romans 8:18-27

● What situation has really tested your patience?

_____

_____

● Many parents find it hard to be patient with their children. How do you manage it?

_____

_____

# RELATE

It can be difficult to get your voice heard when you are the younger sibling. Growing up I developed a stutter because I was so accustomed to people interrupting me. Our son Z always has to wait for his sisters, especially when he wants to say something. My girls talk. There are a lot of words in our house. Some days we hear so many words, we establish a word moratorium. "You've run out of words for the day. Tomorrow is coming soon."

This is one of the byproducts of having four kids.

## IT'S TOO HARD
The older ones are always in conversation with each other, with Noel, or with me. And Zion, because he has grown up listening to a lot of words, has learned a lot of words. He's a verbally expressive kid. But he often has to wait. I remember one day when Zion had waited awhile to tell a story during dinner, quietly stood up on top of his chair and yelled, "I can't wait any longer…IT'S TOO HARD!"

## WAITING FOR OUR KIDS
It is hard to wait. And not just the annoying stuff like waiting for your kids to come out to the car when you've already honked twice. Or waiting for them to finish cleaning their room. It's hard to wait for them to understand a lesson you know will help them win. It's hard to wait for God to convict them about a pattern of behavior. It's hard to wait for them to say, "I'm sorry."

## GOD HELPS US LEARN PATIENCE
Maybe Z is right. This waiting thing, IT'S TOO HARD! Yet patiently waiting is one of the gifts God's Spirit gives us and it is one of the disciplines we are called to as children of God. Paul, after anchoring the people of God to the hope they have in redemption puts it this way in Romans 8:25-26, "But if we hope for what we do not yet have, we wait for it patiently. In the same way, the Spirit helps us in our weakness." Yes, it is hard to wait for what we do not have. But we can trust God to help us remain patient.

## ON THE ROAD

**BEDTIME** The end of the day can serve as an opportune time to recap with your children. As you wind down, create an environment where you can chat with your child. Find a comfy spot on the couch or sit on the bed with them.

## PRESCHOOL Kids

Play a game of waiting this evening. For example: Let's wait for the water to get warm in the bathtub. Let's text a family member and wait for them to reply "Goodnight." Ask your child, "Is it hard to wait?" After they respond, tell them, "The Bible tells us that the Spirit helps us in our weakness. God's Spirit helps us to wait patiently." Together, spend time thinking about the things they will need to wait for tomorrow and pray for God's strength to help them wait patiently.

### FAMILY Fun

Choose a fun word or catchphrase to help each other throughout the day remember to wait patiently. When you notice someone having trouble waiting, use your catchphrase as a fun reminder to rely on the Holy Spirit.

# CHAT Prompts

What are some things everyone has to wait for in our family? What are some things only you have to wait for?

# ELEMENTARY Kids

Find a clock and show it to your child. Together, think of the different times you had to wait throughout the day. Ask your child, "How does waiting feel?" Help them get specific and descriptive. Ask, "Do you wait patiently or impatiently? What does that look like?" After they respond, read Romans 8:25-26 and pray for God's strength to help them wait patiently tomorrow.

# CHAPTER 35

# Kindness

## MEDITATE

*I will tell of the kindnesses of the Lord, the deeds for which he is to be praised, according to all the Lord has done for us—yes, the many good things he has done for Israel, according to his compassion and many kindnesses.* – Isaiah 63:7

Extended passage: Isaiah 63:7-19

## ANTICIPATE

● What is your go-to strategy for handling sickness when it hits your house?

_____

_____

● What was the kindest thing anyone has ever done for your family?

_____

_____

When a cold or flu hits you or one of your kids, it is only a matter of time before everyone in your family gets sick. And you pray, on your knees, that by the time the illness reaches the last family member it does not loop back to the first person who got sick.

When sickness strikes, everyone in our house eventually gets sick and inevitably the virus completes the circuit and gets everyone again. This is why if someone gets the flu in your house, send them to grandma's house. Or move away (you probably have enough food in your cupboards to keep the sick one around until they get better or the house sells). Start making clothes and hats and gloves out of Clorox wipes. Invest heavily in anti-bacterial everything.

## UNEXPECTED THOUGHTFULNESS

Unfortunately, as a parent there is no break when you are sick. No one parents you when you are the sick one in the house. I remember when our whole family was sick at the same time except for our oldest daughter Isabel. Her immune system was the lone holdout to a terrible and violent strain of horribleness. And with my wife unable to get out of bed and the rest of us unable to eat, Isabel served the family in tiny, yet significant ways. She took care of the little ones, changed diapers, played, and put them down for naps. She brought mom and dad ginger ale and ice chips. Isabel's actions were incredibly thoughtful but also profoundly kind.

## OVERWHELMING KINDNESS

If we look closely at the story of God, we find time after time God pours out kindness to his people. In the lavish gifts of the Garden of Eden to the ways God forgave and led Israel to the grace he freely gave by sending his son Jesus to save us, God's kindness is as overwhelming as it is effervescent. We are the sick ones, unable to get past the illness of our own sin, and God's kindness is what saves us and nurses us back to right relationship with our Heavenly Father. Every time.

# ON THE ROAD

The road can be an unkind place, both inside and outside your minivan. We're busy, late, or in a rush. And there is a lot to keep track of when you're getting ready to go somewhere. As a result, our words and our actions can become sharper than normal. Use your time on the road this week to establish a place where kindness can abound and where you can share about the places you see God's kindness showing up in the life of your family.

## PRESCHOOL Kids

Play the Compliment Game while you are driving to your destination. Pay a compliment to your child – be specific and say something kind about their character or actions. Then give your child a turn to compliment you or someone else in the car. If they have a hard time getting started, give them a prompt, like "I love the way you….." or "I really liked it when you…" When you reach your destination, give your child a hug and thank them for their kindness.

## FAMILY Fun

Continue the Compliment Game, paying compliments to people you interact with at work, school, on the playground, or wherever you go this week. Use your words to show kindness to the people. Make cards for teachers, your mail carrier, neighbors, friends – consider who may need to receive kindness this week.

## CHAT **Prompts**

Who is the kindest person you have ever met? Describe the ways they have showed kindness to you. Do you ever try to show people the same type of kindness?

## ELEMENTARY Kids

Invite your child to play the Compliment Game with you. Compliment them by saying something kind and specific about their character or actions. And then give them a turn to compliment you or someone else in the car. If your child seems embarrassed, or struggles to be sincere, give them another chance or a "do-over" and continue the game by modeling kindness and giving out more compliments. When you reach your destination, share what their kindness meant to you, and give them a hug, thanking them for their kindness.

# CHAPTER 36

# The Gift of Goodness

**MEDITATE**

*Let us not become weary in doing good, for at the proper time we will reap a harvest if we do not give up. Therefore, as we have opportunity, let us do good to all people, especially to those who belong to the family of believers.* – Galatians 6:9-10

Extended passage: Galatians 6:1-10

**ANTICIPATE**

● What makes you feel weary as a parent?

_____

_____

● When is it difficult to "do good" for your child or family?

_____

_____

I read an article recently explaining why it's more difficult to raise tweens than infants or toddlers. They maintained that while infants or toddlers are incredibly needy, they also can be quick to reward you with smiles, coos, and sloppy kisses. As children move into their preschool and early elementary years, they become less needy, and then somehow regress as hormones settle in. Suddenly your pre-teen child is incredibly needy (and moody!) and yet they don't compensate with sweet smiles and chubby fists wrapped around your neck as they snuggle in for a hug. Suddenly, what you have is a high-need, low-reward child.

## DON'T BECOME WEARY

Instead of giving us a free pass, Paul exhorts us to *not become weary*. When it's quarter after bedtime and my eleven-year old is crying about her latest crisis. And her sister piggybacks on because she can't handle having to shower again. I know this bedtime battle won't end in them begging for a song and kiss goodnight and so the fight to get there is wearisome and doesn't seem worth the effort. But here I am, called to do good. As parents, that "good" may look like serving our child by praying with them about (another) crisis, and it may look like firmly stating an expectation and following through with a consequence if needed. Friends and comrades: Look. Toward. The. Harvest.

## GOD'S GOODNESS

In between the waves of hormones and streams of irrationality, these big kids who are catapulting towards adulthood faster than their feelings can handle, DO reward us with occasional glimpses of the harvest. This week, my girls have taken out the trash without being asked, they've comforted a sick baby sister, they've offered real help when I was sick myself. And I think that God, in his own goodness, gives me these glimpses so that I do not become weary in doing good. His spirit gives me strength anew to do the things I could never do in my own strength. So when your weariness comes, trust that God's goodness will carry you through, so that you do not become weary in doing good.

Consider the things that make you feel weary. Commit these things to God, asking him to help you look toward the harvest and give you the strength to do the good that needs to be done.

## PRESCHOOL Kids

As you go about the work of "doing good", for your child, focus on the harvest and teach your child to do the same. Let them know, "God has called me to be a good mom/dad, and so I am (helping you by making your breakfast) so that you will someday learn to (help others, too)." Or if the work of "doing good" includes discipline, let them know that you are teaching them to obey so that they grow to love and obey God, too. Affirm the ways that your child is already reflecting Jesus.

## FAMILY Fun

Declare a "Random Act of Kindness" day or even week. Encourage everyone to carry out small acts of kindness for others – begin by brainstorming a list of simple ways to show kindness. Then get started! At the end of the day or week, share how it felt to do good to others.

## CHAT Prompts

What have you done this week that was hard work? How did you feel when you were working hard? How did you feel when you were finished?

# ELEMENTARY Kids

Throughout the day, as you "do good" for your child, share how your role as a parent is to do the work that God has called you to do so that someday, you will reap a harvest – a child that knows and loves God. When you help your child with homework, share that your prayer is that someday will grow to use their knowledge and gifts to serve God and others. When you have to enforce rules, let them know that you do so because you care deeply that they learn to follow God's rules so they can grow closer to him. Take time to notice and affirm ways that your child is becoming more and more like Jesus.

# Faithfulness

## MEDITATE

*The steadfast love of the Lord never ceases; his mercies never come to an end; they are new every morning; great is your faithfulness.*
                                                    – Lamentations 3:22-23 ESV

Extended passage: Lamentations 3:21-26 ESV

## ANTICIPATE

● Think about the passage you just read. How can something that never comes to an end be new every morning?

_____

_____

_____

_____

Growing up I sat with my parents in the adult church service. Every Sunday morning my family woke up, got dressed in our Sunday best (for me it was a three-piece suit and clip on bow tie), grabbed our Bibles, and went to church. Together we sat in the second row on the right side during the first service at Rock Church in Rockford, Illinois. While I often counted the boards lining the vaulted ceiling of the sanctuary during the sermon, I loved it when our congregation sang.

## TEARS FOR FEARS VS AS THE DEER

Our senior pastor led the songs with his wife accompanying him on an old grand piano. I'm sure other elementary kids in the 1980's were listening to Van Halen or Guns N Roses while I was rocking out to "Victory in Jesus," "As the Deer," and "Majesty." But what I loved most was singing hymns. I will always remember the sound of 200 people pulling their hymnal out of the pew rack at the same time and opening to the same page to sing "Holy, Holy, Holy," "All Hail the Power of Jesus' Name," and my favorite "Great Is Thy Faithfulness."

## A HYMN

Great Is Thy Faithfulness is a beautiful hymn written by Thomas Chisolm in 1925. Chisolm was not a pastor or theologian, he was a life insurance agent from New Jersey who struggled with severe health issues. The words of this hymn pull from Lamentations chapter 3 and serve as a testament to the ways God sustains his people. *Great Is Thy faithfulness, O God my Father! There is no shadow of turning with Thee; Though changest not, Thy compassions, they fail not. As Thou hast been Thou forever wilt be.*

## GOD IS FAITHFUL

Faithfulness means God will accomplish everything he says he will accomplish. God will fulfill every promise. God will always and forever be true to his character. And in every moment of our lives, God will faithfully show up. Whether we are celebrating a great victory at home or at work or with our children at school, or whether we are hurting from a painful loss – God is faithful.

# ON THE ROAD

**WAKE UP** Lamentations tells us the mercies of God are "new every morning." Mornings can be tough, right? We have a lot to prepare for the day ahead. This week, take time to reflect on the newness of God's mercies, the steadfastness of his love, and the greatness of his faithfulness each morning together. Intentionally slow down and notice how God is revealing his character to you and your family.

## PRESCHOOL Kids

As your preschooler wakes up this week, encourage them to look outside their window. Take a few minutes to have them to name all of the things they see outside. Ask your child, "Do you see anything new this morning?" Help them identify some of the changes from the previous day (weather, items in the yard, or people outside). Read Lamentations 3:22-23 and remind your child how God's love shows up new every morning.

### FAMILY Fun

Take the words from the Chat Prompt, and together write a prayer to God thanking him for his love using the words you discovered together.

## CHAT **Prompts**

What words come to
your mind about God's love?
Write these words down.

## ELEMENTARY **Kids**

Take a moment together during breakfast and read
Lamentations 3:21-26. Ask your child to listen carefully to
the words with their eyes closed. See if they can find the
words the writer uses to describe God's love, mercy, and
faithfulness (look for "new," "steadfast," "never ceases,"
"never ending," and "great").

# CHAPTER 38

# Gentleness

Extended passage: Matthew 11:25-30

● What burdens does your child carry?

_____

_____

● What does a gentle response look like?

_____

_____

Isabel couldn't wait to start kindergarten. She loved school, and yet at the end of each day she would come home exhausted. I remember her little shoulders hunched under her backpack, heavy with the remains of her lunch and homework and art projects to hang on the fridge. I learned (the hard way, if I'm being honest) to be very gentle with her in the hours between picking her up from the bus stop and settling her into bed. She had poured her energy into the work of learning and listening, navigating playground squabbles, and keeping track of the 137 items in her school supply box all day long. By day's end, she was weary. As her mom, I knew she needed an invitation to come to me with the weight she was carrying. I knew she needed me to offer her rest. To fold gentleness around her weariness.

## WHEN WE ARE WEARY

Some days this came more naturally than others. While she was away at school, I taught a classroom of twenty preschoolers, then came home with Sofia to the endless demands of cleaning and laundry and meal prep. Sometimes, I didn't feel like being gentle. I felt like tending to my own needs and offloading my own burdens. As parents, self-care is certainly important, but we don't always have the luxury of practicing self-care on our own timetable. Thank God we are not called to do the overwhelming tasks of caring for these small but very needy children in our own strength. He has promised to help us do this work he has called us to.

## JESUS PROMISES REST

Jesus's words call to us in those moments when this holy work of carrying our child's heavy loads becomes too heavy of a load for us to bear. "Become my servants and learn from me," he says. And in the same way I took my little girl's backpack from her tiny shoulders, he gently takes the load we can no longer carry. He teaches us gentleness by extending gentleness. When we are weary, he offers us the gift of rest, and once rested we can turn and with gentleness, offer our children rest when they need it most.

# ON THE ROAD

**AT HOME** This week, take notice of when your child is weary. Consider the work it takes for them to follow directions, ask for help, wait patiently for their turn, and resist the temptation to demand their way. Notice and affirm your child's hard work, and strive to be like Jesus: a gentle teacher.

## PRESCHOOL Kids

If your child attends preschool, let them know when they come home that you are proud of how hard they worked today. If they are home all day, stop throughout the day and praise how hard they are working. When your child is weary, they may show it by losing their temper or dissolving into tears. Respond with gentleness. Scoop them up and offer to help carry their burden – help them clean up, make a snack, or settle down with them for some rest time. Use gentle words and affection to let them know that you are there to help when they are weary.

## FAMILY Fun

Practice gentleness by playing a game where you choose an activity (talking, eating, building a tower, singing, giving a backrub) and then do that activity VERY gently. Talk about how Jesus will help us treat each other with gentleness, even when it's hard.

## CHAT **Prompts**

What did you do today that was hard work? What are some things I do that help you? Remind your child that Jesus offers us the gift of gentleness so that we can be gentle and help others.

## ELEMENTARY **Kids**

When your child comes home from school, tell them you're proud of how they worked hard and share that hard work can make you weary. Explain what it looks like and how it feels when you're weary – maybe you're short-tempered, or you crave peace and quiet, or you need a chance to burn off some steam by going for a walk. Ask your child what it feels like when they are weary, and what they need from you. Respond to your child with gentle words and affection. Let them know that when they are weary, you want to help.

# CHAPTER 39

# Self-control

**MEDITATE**

*God gave us his Spirit. And the Spirit doesn't make us weak and fearful. Instead, the Spirit gives us power and love. He helps us control ourselves.* – 2 Timothy 1:7 NIRV

Extended passage: 2 Timothy 1:6-10

**ANTICIPATE**

● What do you enjoy more: musicals or drama?

_____

_____

● When is it difficult for you to maintain self-control?

_____

_____

## RELATE

Isabel and Sofia enjoy theater. Throughout their elementary years, they have been in several musical productions and wanted to audition for a creative arts performing academy. The process was excruciatingly difficult. As they prepared, I decided to ask my friend Jay to watch and critique their audition piece. Jay has significant experience as an actor and director, so I knew the experience would be worthwhile albeit challenging. Jay is kind of a tough teacher even though he has the heart of a grandparent.

## WINCE

The girls were used to teachers and coaches who lavished them with encouragement. Jay asked them to perform their audition piece and they timidly walked into the living room and stumbled through their pieces. He quickly interjected, "Learning your lines girls, that's the easy part! I should send you home right now and you can come back when you learned your lines!"

I could see Isabel and Sofia wince.

## THE SECRET WEAPON

Jay wasn't finished. "Don't come out in front of the audience with your head down and your eyes on the floor. Walk out with your head high, take a deep breath, and speak to a thousand people. If you're afraid, stay home. Discipline yourself." In 45 minutes I saw different kids emerge. The girls worked even harder on their auditions and we were all proud of what they accomplished. Later, I asked the girls what they learned from Jay. Their response was simple: an actor's secret weapon is self-control.

## THE GIFT

Paul talks to Timothy about self-control. He prods him to stand firm as a leader with confidence by the power of God's Spirit. Because in today's culture, we are encouraged to say "yes" to everything. But controlling ourselves allows us to say no and to teach our children to do the same. Thankfully, we do not need to rely on our own strength to turn towards what is good. The Holy Spirit helps us at every turn, crossroads, and decision point.

SELF-CONTROL

# ON THE ROAD

**WAKE UP** Mornings are often a time when self-control is needed but difficult to exercise. As everyone rushes to brush teeth, get dressed, grab breakfast and get started with their day, it's easier to demand our way than it is to wait patiently.

## PRESCHOOL Kids

Before breakfast, place a bowl of something tasty – and tempting – in the middle of the table. Tell your child that the food looks soooo delicious, and that you want to eat it all and right away! But you have to wait until (everyone comes to the table, the dishwasher is empty, the dog is fed, etc. Choose just one thing to wait for). Explain that it will take self-control, but that you know God promises to give us self-control. When you sit down to breakfast, make a big deal about how delicious the food is and how glad you had self-control and waited together.

## FAMILY Fun

Play a game to practice self-control. Name an action (run, jump, dance, etc.) and have your child do that action until you shout: Freeze! When they freeze, compliment them on their self-control.

## CHAT **Prompts**

When do you have a hard time controlling yourself? How do you hurt yourself and others when you don't use self-control? How can we pray for you – where or when do you need God to give you self-control?

## ELEMENTARY **Kids**

Let your child know the night before that you'll be having something special for breakfast – share what it is and how much you're looking forward to it. Then remind your child of what needs to be done before you can enjoy breakfast together. When you wake your child up, remind them of the special breakfast, and say a quick prayer together that God will give you self-control as you get ready for breakfast. Once you sit down to breakfast, share how glad you are that God gave you both self-control.

# CHAPTER 40

# God Will Never Leave You

## MEDITATE

*Joshua, no one will be able to stand up against you as long as you live. I will be with you, just as I was with Moses. I will never leave you. I will never desert you.* – Joshua 1:5 (NIRV)

Extended passage: Joshua 1:1-9

## ANTICIPATE

● Describe a time when you felt God's presence and knew that he was with you.

_____

_____

● How do you respond when your child is afraid of being alone?

_____

_____

# RELATE

I woke up one morning to the sound of my ten-year old daughter screaming that her leg hurt and she couldn't walk. We rushed Isabel to the hospital where ER doctors performed tests to determine what was wrong. Some of the tests were painful – I will never forget holding Isabel down while the doctors worked quickly, tears streaming down my face as I told her I was right there and I wouldn't leave. Months later the pain was better but not gone, and I took her to another hospital for an MRI. This time, I was pregnant and so I wasn't allowed to stay with her. I remember sitting in the waiting room, tears once again streaming down my face, hating that I couldn't be with my little girl. And so I prayed that she would feel deeply that God was with her, that she would be comforted knowing that he would never leave her and she wasn't alone.

## A GREAT LEADER

Joshua had watched the presence of God go before his people. He had seen how God was with Moses as he led the Israelites. And now it was Joshua's turn to lead the people into the Promised Land. The fact that God instructs Joshua over and over again to be brave, tells me that Joshua must have wrestled with fear. Maybe Joshua felt alone or maybe he just felt overwhelmed with the task at hand. But God promised that he would never leave or desert him. Joshua was one of the greatest leaders Israel had ever known because he put his faith in a God who was with him.

## WORDS OF COMFORT

Sometimes our children have to face the fear of being alone. We tuck them into bed, drop them off at school, send them off to camp, wait outside their hospital room… we know that part of raising children is letting them do these things without us. But we can teach them that they are never alone. I have been amazed at how that promise has comforted my children snuggled in their beds or staying still for an MRI. God's words to Joshua are just as true today – his promise to never leave or desert us is a comfort we can send with our children wherever the journey leads them.

# ON THE ROAD

**BEDTIME** Putting our children to bed is an excellent opportunity to begin teaching them to trust in God's promise to never leave or desert them. Use this time to settle their hearts and remember that God is with them always.

## PRESCHOOL Kids

Your preschooler may be adept in postponing bedtime with an arsenal of creative methods. A request for one more drink or story or snuggle may be a plea for attention, but it also likely stems from a natural fear of being alone. Tonight, read Joshua 1:5 as a blessing over your child. As you leave their room, pray that God's presence will comfort your child when they feel alone or afraid.

### FAMILY Fun

God's presence is like a light in the darkness – no matter how dark it is, the light will show. Take turns bringing a flashlight into a dark room where you are all alone. Close the door then turn on the flashlight and say, "God will never leave me!"

## CHAT Prompts

Why do you think we sometimes feel nervous or afraid of being alone? How can we remember God's promise?

# ELEMENTARY Kids

While older children are less fearful of being alone (at least outwardly), they still sometimes struggle with fear, especially at night when it's dark and their imaginations run wild. When you put your child to bed, remind them that they are not alone because God promises to always be with them. They may have questions about how God can be with them when they can't see him, or how he can be in more than one place at once. Feel free to let them know that you wonder about those things too, but that Scripture tells us that even though we don't understand all the mysteries of who God is, we can still trust in what God says. Read Joshua 1:5 over them as a blessing and pray together, thanking God for his promise to never leave or desert us.

# CHAPTER 41

# God Will Come Back for You

 **MEDITATE**

*There are many rooms in my Father's house. If this were not true, would I have told you that I am going there? Would I have told you that I would prepare a place for you there? 3 If I go and do that, I will come back. And I will take you to be with me. Then you will also be where I am.*

– John 14:2-3

Extended passage: John 14:1-4

 **ANTICIPATE**

● What do you enjoy about traveling?

_____

_____

● What do you enjoy about coming home after a trip?

_____

_____

## RELATE

Not that long ago I had visions of becoming a grown up and traveling on airplanes to big cities, eating local delicacies, visiting the best places, and staying in fancy hotels. I thought traveling would be the most exciting, exotic experience. Now that I have a job requiring a little bit of travel, I can assure you – I either have not grown up yet or travel is not glamourous.

## WHY ARE YOU GOING AWAY

Most of the time, travel is just waiting in line with really frustrated people. When I started traveling with regularity, I wanted Zion to understand the change. So we started reading a children's book about airports and modes of transportation. I was able to share how I would experience nearly every kind of travel in his book in my new job. But Zion's response surprised me when he asked, "Dad, why are you going away?"

## PURPOSE

For Zion, knowing where I was going was helpful but the reason behind my leaving was far more important. I began to consider the purpose behind my travel. I felt God's calling on my life to help people who work with kids and families in the church, so every trip to speak or visit a ministry leader was tied to a mission. I invited Z to pray for me during my trips, to ask God to help me accomplish my mission, and save me a big hug for when I came back home (because I always come back home).

## THE GREATEST ROAD TRIP

Throughout the book of John, Jesus reveals his identity and mission to the disciples and they struggle to come to grips with it. Finally, in John 14, Jesus lays everything out for them and makes three things clear. First, he is going to leave (this is a difficult truth). Second, he is going to prepare a place for them (this is a profound mission). Third, he is coming back to get them (this is a beautiful promise). Moms and dads, Jesus took the greatest road trip of all time when he died and rose again for you. And you can take heart because he is coming back for you.

# ON THE ROAD

It's hard to talk about this promise of God because it is difficult to imagine. How will God, whom we have never seen, return to earth and restore all things? Even though this is a tough topic, it is a hope-filled promise. As you head into this week's activities and discussions during your drive time, ask God to give you wisdom to navigate the time with the right words. And if your child asks a question you do not know the answer to, rest assured – it's okay! Let them know you will work with them to see what God's Word has to say.

## PRESCHOOL Kids

Describe a few different trips with your child (going to preschool, church, or the grocery store). Together, walk through all the steps in the trip (getting ready, getting in the car, driving, going inside, coming back to the car, and coming home). Highlight for your child, "What happens at the end of every trip? We come back home." Read John 14:2-3 and remind your child, "God is coming back for us."

## FAMILY Fun

Play an epic game of Hide and Go Seek. Have your child hide and you find them. Bring some pillows with you so when you find them, you can hide together for awhile and talk about how God is coming back to find us.

Ask the following questions.
"Can we see Jesus? Where is
Jesus right now? Do you think
he is coming back? What will
happen when he does?"

# ELEMENTARY Kids

Have your child name five different places they would love
to visit someday. Ask them, "What will you do when you visit?
What do you want to see?" Then ask, "What will happen at
the end of the trip?" Have your child read John 14:2-3 and
ask, "What do you notice about this verse?" Let them know,
"God is coming back for you and for me. One day we will
see him face-to-face. How does that make you feel?"

# CHAPTER 42

# God Promises to Forgive

## MEDITATE

*But God is faithful and fair. If we admit that we have sinned, he will forgive us our sins. He will forgive every wrong things we have done. He will make us pure.* – 1 John 1:9 (NIRV)

Extended passage: 1 John 5-10

## ANTICIPATE

- Is your child more likely to admit to or deny their wrongdoing?

_____

_____

- Think of a time that you confessed your sin and truly felt the gift of God's forgiveness.

_____

_____

## RELATE

I found the Mother Daughter journal – a special book Sofi and I use to write notes to each other – propped up on my pillow, a ribbon marking the page meant for me to read. Sofi had written to tell me that Isabel had been saying some cruel and hurtful things to her, so we called Isabel in to confront her.

## THE TRUTH COMES OUT

We showed her the words her sister had written, then offered her a moment to determine if she would tell us the truth. This has become a practice in our home – before we ask our children to admit to wrongdoing, we first ask them if they are ready to tell the truth. Something about committing to truth prepares their heart for confession. Once Isabel committed to the truth, tears began to flow, and her confession bubbled over. Because she loves her sister deeply, she was overwhelmed by guilt over her actions. And because she desires our approval, she was heartbroken that she had disappointed us. We spoke about her words and we administered discipline that would help correct her course because our desire is for her to get back on the right path. Most importantly, we forgave her. We offered her the gift of restoration – loving her as deeply as if she'd never spoken the words she now regretted. When we forgive our children, we don't ignore their wrongdoing, but we don't let their mistakes define our relationship or become their identity.

## FAITHFUL FORGIVENESS

God offers us this same gift. When the ugliness in our hearts spills into our words and actions, we are invited to confess. So often we want to hide our sin. Whether by justifying it or denying it, we keep in the dark what God longs for us to bring into the light. Confessed sin is powerless – powerless to define us, to hinder us, to keep us from an intimate relationship with our Father. Confessed sin always results in forgiveness from a fair and faithful God. Even when consequences follow, our course correction will put us back on the right path, in right relationship with a God who guides us forward in love.

**AT HOME** In order to receive forgiveness, our children must first choose to tell the truth and admit their mistake. As parents, we need to model this ourselves. When our children see us admit our need for forgiveness, then ask for and receive forgiveness, they will learn to do the same.

## PRESCHOOL Kids

Preschoolers don't fully understand the difference between real and pretend, so when they make a mistake, they will often tell a story that tells what they think we want to hear – or what they want to be true. Preschoolers often exclaim, "I didn't mean to!" which usually means that they regret or feel badly about their choice. Teach your preschooler about confession by modeling it at home. This week when you sin in front of your child, stop and confess – show your preschooler that telling the truth the way it is, instead of the way you want it to be, is safe and even positive. Use simple words to admit your sin and say you're sorry to God. Then let your child know how good it feels to know that God forgives and loves you.

## FAMILY Fun

At bedtime, invite your child to confess any sins they committed that day – but first model this yourself. If your child has a hard time remembering, simply invite them to ask God's forgiveness for any bad choices they may have made and try again the next day. Thank God for forgiving our sins, and celebrate that tomorrow is a fresh start.

## CHAT Prompts

Why is it so hard to admit when
we've made the wrong choice?
Why is it easier to lie
or hide the truth?

# ELEMENTARY Kids

Older children have a stronger grasp on truth and lies, but they are often motivated by a desire for approval or a fear of punishment to hide their sin. Teach them to embrace confession and receive forgiveness by modeling it yourself. Talk about the power of truth and confession in your own life; be honest about your temptation to hide your sin and how God is faithful to forgive. The next time you need to confront your child about their sin, first ask if they are ready to choose truth. Then guide them to confess their sin to God and receive his forgiveness. Celebrate the truth that was told and the forgiveness that was given.

**CHAPTER 43**

# God Will Love You with Everlasting Love

*The Lord appeared to us in the past, saying: "I have loved you with an everlasting love; I have drawn you with unfailing kindness*

– Jeremiah 31:3

Extended passage: Jeremiah 31:1-6

● What do you do for Valentine's Day?

_____

_____


● How do you express love to the people around you?

_____

_____

Most of my elementary school years were spent as a homeschooler. While this may conjure up images of a country family knitting our own clothes out of homespun cotton and churning butter, I can assure you I never learned to knit. I was more a cross-stitch guy.

## VALENTINE'S DAY

As a homeschooler in a class of one, Valentine's Day was not filled with the exchange of themed cards and small pieces of candy. On Valentine's Day, I gave myself a hug and went about my day. My older children experienced something different. During their elementary years they attended schools where the exchange of Valentine's Day cards was a big deal.

## I LOVE YOU

Now when your children learn to write, something changes. The words they express are trapped in time. And when my kids learned to write, they started to share Valentine's Day cards with me. And while most of the time, parenting is a thankless job – sometimes you read words from your children that you never forget. My daughter Sofie wrote to me once, "You're the greatest dad I know. I love you." My daughter Isabel once wrote, "I love you more than anything." I turned both cards into cross-stitch patterns. Not really.

## EVERLASTING LOVE

Jeremiah reminds the exiled people of Israel of some of the most life-giving words God ever spoke. "I have loved you with an everlasting love." The love of God reaches beyond the bounds of time. God loved even before Israel existed. The apostle Paul picks up on this language and applies it to each of us in his letter to the Ephesians when he writes, "For he chose us in him before the foundation of the world...In love he predestined us for adoption to sonship through Jesus Christ" (Ephesians 1:4-5). The love God has for you goes far beyond the cards shared between 3rd graders on Valentine's Day, it eclipses the love a child shares with their parents, and it even surpasses the great love each parent has for their child. God loves you and this love is everlasting!

**I LOVE** Everyone expresses love in unique ways. Some parents can easily put their love into words. Others are more comfortable showing their love through action. Whatever style fits your personality, make it abundantly clear to your family this week: "I love you. I am so proud of you." As you portray love audibly and tangibly to your family, you echo the great love God has for you.

## PRESCHOOL Kids

This week, prepare a card for your preschooler to give them when they wake up. For extra fun, give hints through their morning routine so they can find the card during breakfast. Use the card as a way to speak affirming, loving words over your child. Include the verse from Jeremiah inside.

### FAMILY Fun

Draw pictures together expressing your love for God!

## CHAT Prompts

What makes you feel loved
(I know you love me because
you…)? How do you enjoy
showing love to others?

## ELEMENTARY Kids

This week, write your child a note that will encourage
them throughout the day. Think through their daily
schedule (especially if they are in school) and come up
with loving ways to inspire them. For instance, if they have
a game in the afternoon include how proud you are of the
way they work hard for their team and how excited you
are to cheer them on. Don't forget to include Jeremiah
31:3 inside.

# CHAPTER 44

# God Works for the Good of Those Who Love Him

*And we know that in all things God works for the good of those who love him, who have been called according to his purpose.*

– Romans 8:28

Extended passage: Romans 8:28-30

● Describe a situation where you felt hopeless.

_____

_____


● What's your typical response when you face a difficult problem?

_____

_____

## RELATE

Every family has unique Thanksgiving traditions. In our family, we celebrate two rounds of Thanksgiving (one with each set of grandparents), we break a wishbone, and we decorate my grandmother's Christmas Tree. Every year, I anxiously anticipate each tradition. Smelling roasted turkey, sausage stuffing, and green bean casserole. Waiting for the wishbone to dry. Eating lemon meringue pie.

## ONE TISSUE

But Thanksgiving 2014 was different than every other Thanksgiving because the day before the celebration, my foster sister was placed in a new home. My family was devastated beyond words. My grandparents were heartbroken. And I was trying to accept that this was part of God's great plan for me, my foster sister, and my family. After we dropped off my foster sister to her new home, I was speechless. I didn't know what to feel. I remember getting into the van and my mom sat in the backseat with my sister and me. All of us were all blinded with tears. "I managed to save one tissue for all of us to share!" mom said. We all laughed, despite the sadness.

## ALL THINGS FOR GOOD

When our van finally pulled into our driveway, my heart was heavy with the weight of change. As we walked inside our house, even with 5 people inside, it just felt empty. I had so many questions ringing inside me like an echo chamber. What will happen to my foster sister? Will she be okay? Will I remember her? Then suddenly our doorbell rung and we slowly went to find out who was at the front door. All we saw was a basket of goodies with the movie "A Charlie Brown Thanksgiving," a loaf of bread, a bag of jelly beans, and popcorn. And in a moment things were just a little different. We popped popcorn, poured jelly beans into a bowl, and toasted bread. And the night before Thanksgiving was filled with laughter and buttery toast, despite the difficulty we faced just a few hours before. Even on our hardest day as a family, God worked for our good.

# ON THE ROAD

God promises in Romans 8:28 that no matter what comes your way, God is in control and will ultimately transform your difficulty into something good. Are you facing any difficult situations right now? Are your children facing a tough time at school or in their activities? How might you point them towards the promise in Romans 8:28? This week, take a walk together. Getting outside of your house will be good for you and provide space to talk and reflect.

## PRESCHOOL Kids

As you walk with your preschooler, point them towards the good work God has accomplished. Ask your child, "What things do you see that change from season to season? Does the sky change? Do the trees change? Do you see any plants that grow fruit or vegetables?" When your child responds, follow up by asking, "What do you like about that?" Remind your child that God does good work and he allows us to enjoy it.

### FAMILY Fun

Make dinner together and assign each family member a task to fulfill. Enjoy the good work you've accomplished together!

## CHAT Prompts

Ask your child, "Is it hard to know God is always with us, thinking about what's best for us? Why or why not?"

# ELEMENTARY Kids

During your walk, invite your child to talk about anything difficult they might be facing. Check in with them. Peek under the hood. You will need to ask at least three questions before you get underneath the surface. For example, you can start with, "Tell me about your friends these days. Who are you hanging out with? What do you like about them? What do you do together? Is everything going good between you?" As you dig into these areas, take time on your walk to recall Romans 8:28. Read the verse and pray it over your child's difficult situation.

# CHAPTER 45

# God Will Meet Your Needs

My God will meet all your needs. He will meet them in keeping with his wonderful riches. These riches come to you because you belong to Christ Jesus.  – Philippians 4:19 NIRV

Extended passage: Philippians 4:14-20

● What worry keeps you up at night?

_____

_____

● How do you respond when God takes care of you in a big way?

_____

_____

My children love food. The foods they ate as babies changed over time. As 4th and 5th graders, they would never eat a pouch filled with pureed carrots. However, pouches with applesauce are somehow still ok. Why are we so obsessed with putting liquified food in handheld bags?

## MISSING MEALS

A few years ago, my daughter Sofie became intensely fixated on the food she was going to eat. She made sure we ate. She had a paper calendar she would check off three times a day after she ate. When mealtime was coming, she would ask no less than 10 times what we were going to eat. When I asked Sofie about meals, her food calendar, and all the questions she replied, "I'm just worried we're going to miss a meal." Moms and dads I promise you, I do not miss meals. Other parents might get busy enough to miss a meal. I am not one of those parents. I eat every meal. If anything, I find extra meals to eat. But Sofie wasn't thinking about me, her question came from a deeper place. She was really asking me, "Will we have what we need?"

## GOD PROVIDES

Anxiety causes us to question even the things we can count on. Relationships. The love of others. Motives. Outcomes. God's provision. Yet God promises to supply to us the things we need. Not some of the time. All of the time. And this promise stands in contrast to the things we might desire. God provides for our needs. We need not question his motives, doubt his love, or wonder whether or not he can or will come through. Paul, the writer of Philippians, saw it happen as he was sitting in a Roman prison and the people of Philippi sent him money. No door, no chain, no guard can stop God's giving hand.

## OUR RESPONSE

And Philippians 4:20 captures the proper response to God's work on our behalf: humble worship. Paul says, "Give glory to our God the Father for ever and ever. Amen." When our needs are met, we do not accept the credit or pat ourselves on the back. We just give God praise, over and over again.

JANUARY
21

## ON THE ROAD

**BEDTIME** This week, become a master noticer. Have you ever stopped to consider just how much you have? It's easy if you've moved to a new home recently. But often, we forget the many ways God provides for us. Start to recognize and call out the needs being met in your life and in your child's life. Where is God providing? What is God providing? As you notice God's provision for you and your family, take time to specifically give God praise.

## PRESCHOOL Kids

As you get ready for bedtime, name a need and have your child think of some examples. Say, "You need food. What are some of your favorite foods? You need love. Who loves you? You need a safe place to stay. What keeps you safe in our house? You need to stay warm when it's cold. What keeps you warm at night?" Finish by thanking God for the many ways he meets your preschooler's needs.

### FAMILY Fun

Play a cause discovery game together. Start with the question, "What is your favorite meal?" Name the ingredients in that meal and try to trace where each ingredient came from.

## CHAT Prompts

Have you ever wondered if God will take care of you or your family? Share a story of when you wondered if God would care for you and he came through.

# ELEMENTARY Kids

Read Philippians 4:19 with your child. Tell them, "God has enough to take care of us. He meets our needs from his riches." Ask your child, "What are some of the needs you have this week?" Help them think beyond basic physical needs like food or clothes and consider what needs they have that would take more to meet than they have available. Together, invite God to meet those needs.

**CHAPTER 46**

# God Promises Wisdom

## MEDITATE

*If any of you lacks wisdom, you should ask God, who gives generously to all without finding fault, and it will be given to you.* – James 1:5

Extended passage: James 1:2-18

## ANTICIPATE

- When have you acted without wisdom? What were the consequences?

_____

_____

- What decisions, relationships, or problems are you facing that require wisdom?

_____

_____

## RELATE

We were sitting at the dinner table when I opened the History tab on my laptop and came across a list of websites that are intended to get people to click, not learn anything – you know the kind. They masquerade as innocent children's games but they're intended to elicit personal information. My girls, who had been using my computer, were afraid they were in trouble but sure they had done nothing wrong. In those moments, I was torn between explaining the real and horrible dangers that the internet presents, and protecting their innocence by brushing it under the rug. This wasn't the first or last moment I felt overwhelmed and under-equipped to teach and protect my children. But thankfully I learned early on to ask God for wisdom.

## TAKE A MOMENT

I often find myself pausing in mid-conversation to pray and ask God for wisdom. Sometimes I do this alone; other times I invite my children to pray with me. They know that I don't know all the answers, that I make mistakes, that my experience isn't enough to equip me with all that I need to guide them along the journey. But they also know that God has everything that we need, and that he will graciously and generously give us wisdom whenever we ask.

## SEEK GOD

Before James shares God's promise to give us wisdom, he explains that trials are inevitable, and that in fact we should consider them pure joy for the work they do in maturing our faith. We often find ourselves in need of wisdom when we are facing a trial or difficult situation. Whether it's a parenting issue that we are trying to navigate, a relationship we are trying to mend, or a decision we are wrestling with, our search for wisdom often arises out of a struggle that threatens to overtake us. We find ourselves overwhelmed because we don't know where to turn. This can be especially terrifying as a parent, because so much is at stake in the hearts and minds of our children. But when we find ourselves in a difficult place, we can seek God and trust in his promise to give us wisdom whenever we ask.

# ON THE ROAD

**AT HOME** Our kids need to know that we don't have all the answers and that's ok, because we trust in a God who does, and who promises to give us wisdom. They learn this by watching us go to God for help. When we ask God for wisdom, we teach our children to do the same.

## PRESCHOOL Kids

While preschoolers know right from wrong, they often struggle with impulse and how to apply their knowledge in real-life situations. They know that stealing is wrong, but they will take their friend's toy because they want to play with it. This week, when you notice your child struggling to make the right choice, pause and pray with them. Ask God to give them the wisdom to make the right choice.

## FAMILY Fun

Brainstorm a list of decisions your family will have to make this week. Every day, choose one decision from the list and pray that God will give wisdom to make the right choice. As you make decisions with God's help, celebrate his promise to give us wisdom whenever we ask.

## CHAT Prompts

What is wisdom? How can God's promise to give us wisdom help us in a difficult situation?

# ELEMENTARY Kids

School-aged children often face more complex problems that don't always have a simple "right or wrong" answer. Give your child the time and attention they need to talk about difficult things they've heard or seen at school, playing with friends, or surfing the internet. Instead of solving their problems, read James 1:5 and invite them to pray with you for wisdom. Follow up with them later to see how God gave them wisdom when facing a problem.

# CHAPTER 47

# God Will Teach You All Things

## MEDITATE

*But the Advocate, The Holy Spirit, whom the Father will send in my name, will teach you all things and will remind you of everything I have said to you.* – John 14:26

Extended passage: John 14:15-31

## ANTICIPATE

● Think of a time that the Holy Spirit reminded you of a verse or passage when you really needed it.

_____

_____

● What are you facing that you feel ill-equipped to handle? What do you need the Holy Spirit to teach you, and how can you rely on him to do so?

_____

_____

This fall, we turned our sunroom into a preschool room for Zion. We hung posters, organized art supplies, and set up centers. I told him that we'd start by learning letters and once he had learned all the letters he'd have the power to read, and now he repeats this to everyone who will listen. We've been at it for several months, and slowly he's learning his letters and how they come together to make words. He wrote his first word - "MOM" (be still my heart) and he was so very proud. Sometimes he forgets something we learned that week and I remind him what the letter says, or what number he's pointing to, or what the name of our book was. I teach, and he learns, and our preschool days are something that we both love and look forward to.

## MUCH TO LEARN

Our faith journey is a lot like our sunroom preschool. We begin, knowing very little of what we have to learn. God prepares our hearts for the things he plans to teach us and we start out wide-eyed at how much there is to know. But over time, he patiently reveals truth to us through his Word, and as we learn more about who God is and what he has done, his story comes together in our hearts. And then sometimes we forget - no matter how far we've come, doubts and worry can cloud our minds and that is when we need the Holy Spirit to remind us of what God has said.

## LEARNING TO TEACH

This promise - that God's Spirit will teach us all things and remind us of what God has said - is a promise that I rely on every day. This work of training my children to know and love God is more than I can do on my own. Sometimes they have questions I can't answer, problems I can't solve, or behaviors I can't handle. In those moments, I trust in God's promise. I step away and ask him to teach me, so that I can teach my child. I take a moment to ask him to remind me of his words, so that I can speak them to my child. When I remember that God is teaching and I am learning, this journey of raising my children is one that I can love and look forward to.

# ON THE ROAD

Time in the car is great for connecting. Jesus promised that the Holy Spirit would "remind you of everything I've said to you." I've found that in difficult times, God's Spirit brings to mind a verse from Scripture, often one I learned as a child. This week, take advantage of your time in the car to memorize Jesus's promise with your child.

## PRESCHOOL Kids

Give your child a moment to calm down. Talk about their sins Tell your child that Jesus promised that the Holy Spirit would teach us all things – everything we need to know, God's Spirit will teach us. It's our job to listen and learn. Share that Jesus also promised that his Spirit would remind us of Jesus's word, but the Bible also teaches us that we need to read and memorize God's Word, and he will remind us of those words when we need them. Together, memorize John 14:26. (You could also memorize a shortened version: "The Holy Spirit... will teach you all things and will remind you of everything I have said to you.")

## FAMILY Fun

Have each family member choose a favorite Bible verse (if they can't think of one, choose a few, and allow them to pick a favorite). Have them write their verse on a notecard (help younger children with this). Place these verses in a place where they will be seen often, and memorize them together.

## CHAT **Prompts**

What is a favorite verse from
the Bible that you have read
or learned? How has that
verse helped you?

# ELEMENTARY **Kids**

Share that Jesus promised that the Holy Spirit would teach
us all things, and that as we read and study God's Word,
he teaches us what we need to know. He also reminds
us of God's words when we need them. Invite them to
memorize John 14:26 with you, and encourage them to
be listening to what the Holy Spirit wants to teach them.

# CHAPTER 48

# God Will Help You

 **MEDITATE**

*"For I am the Lord your God who takes hold of your right hand and says to you, Do not fear; I will help you."* – Isaiah 41:13 (NIV)

Extended passage: Isaiah 41:11-14

 **ANTICIPATE**

● What were you afraid of as a child?

_____

_____

● Under what circumstances does your child wake up in the middle of the night and come into your room?

_____

_____

## RELATE

Once my kids moved into their own rooms, I never dreamed they would ever show back up in my room after I went to sleep. But one night, there was daughter Isabel, two inches from my face, whispering "I can't sleep."

## WAKING UP

Besides the fact that nothing is more terrifying than being whispered creepily to in the middle of a REM cycle, I knew I had an opportunity in my hands. So my carefully crafted response to Bel was, "Go. Back. To. Bed...Please." When you're asleep, you're not exactly in the best frame of mind to articulate anything. And the midnight wake ups kept happening as my kids were scared due to a bad dream or a storm rolling through. Eventually, I learned to give a different response. I would hold their hands, ask them to pray, and send them off to bed. After this happened a few times, it suddenly stopped. Nights were filled with rest once again. After a few months, one of the girls came into our bedroom and whispered, "I had a bad dream." I started to go into my prayer response and she interrupted me. "Wait, I actually need help. I thought you were mom." Ouch. It turns out, my wife was holding the kids, calming their fears, and walking them hand in hand back to bed night after night.

## DO NOT FEAR

In Isaiah the prophet proclaims a promise of God to his people. In the face of fear, when we stare our enemy in the eyes, God helps us. He holds us and looks into our eyes and says, "Do not fear." What gracious help. God does not sleepily say, "Go back to bed." I love how God uses his hands to help. You always hold a baby, but as your children age you hold them less and less. Not so with God. Moms and dads take note of God's example and hold your children. Their age is immaterial. Whether they like it or not, hold them. When God holds us he helps us. When God holds us we become freed from fear. When God holds us our lives are filled with impenetrable hope.

# ON THE ROAD

**WAKE UP** Isaiah captures God using two things to send a message to his people: his voice and his touch. In the same way God uses these to encourage his children, both are incredible tools for you as a parent to intentionally communicate truth and love to your family. This week, make sure you use your voice and your touch during wake up time as you help your child get ready for each day.

## PRESCHOOL Kids

Make it a point to be there when your preschooler wakes up. This might require some preparation the night before, but you can do it! As you say "Good morning," emphasize how much you love them and are proud of them. You can never say this enough. Then exert extra effort to help them prepare for the day ahead.

### FAMILY Fun

Plan a sleepover night. The kids can join you in your room or vice versa. Take time to hold your kids!

## CHAT **Prompts**

Talk about fears. Share
the fears you had growing
up and what helped you
overcome them.

# ELEMENTARY **Kids**

As our kids get older, we naturally expect more out of
them. This is healthy! But this morning, intentionally help
your kids with some of the items in the morning routine
you would typically rely on them to accomplish. Let
them know, "Hey, I wanted to help you this morning just
because I love you." Lend a helping hand and try to create
some margin in the morning so you can read Isaiah 41:11-
14 together.

# CHAPTER 49

# God Trains Those He Loves

## MEDITATE

*The Lord trains those he loves. He is like a father who trains the son he is pleased with.* – Proverbs 3:12 (NIRV)

Extended passage: Proverbs 3:11-18

## ANTICIPATE

● What is something that you have trained for?

_____

_____

● In what ways has God trained you along your faith journey?

_____

_____

# RELATE

When the girls were eight and nine, they begged to train for a 5k with me. In the beginning, there was more walking than running and everyone was having fun. But as the running time stretched and the walking time waned, the girls were less and less motivated to finish training. Sometimes I was able to encourage them to keep going, and other times I had to push them along, but in the end we trained and ran that race together. As we crossed the finish line, we grabbed hands and in that moment, all of the training was worth it. My girls would later share that finishing that race was one of their favorite memories. Halfway through, I could not have convinced them that they were training for one of the best moments of their lives – they had to finish to experience it for themselves. But I had to be willing to keep them on track, pushing them to train so we could cross that finish line together.

## THE GOAL

One thing I learned from training for that race with my girls, was that the goal of training was always to cross the finish line. I pushed them to go further because I knew they could. I corrected their form because I knew it would cause them pain. I encouraged them when they were weary because I knew it would give them strength. I knew that finishing that race would be an incredible moment – not just for me, but more importantly, for them.

## THE FINISH LINE

God promises to train (other versions use the word "discipline") *those he loves*. Sometimes we veer off course, and God disciplines us out of love to correct that course...always focused on the finish line. He sets the example that we as parents must follow. We are charged with training our children to run the ultimate race – a life of faith that brings us to the finish line of eternity with Jesus. As we run this race ourselves, we can trust in a God who promises to train us, even as we train our children, so that one day we can finish the race together.

# ON THE ROAD

**AT HOME** Consider something you and your child can train for together. Maybe it's running a race, or maybe it's beating a high score in a video game. Whatever you choose, commit to training together with the goal of crossing the finish line.

## PRESCHOOL Kids

Ask your preschooler to name something that they want to be better at. Give them a few ideas if they need help, but make sure that you choose something that has an end goal or finish line. Then make a plan to train together. Create a sticker chart or calendar and mark off the days you train. If your child wants to quit, encourage them to continue, helping them along the way if needed. When you cross your finish line, celebrate together! Then read Proverbs 3:12 and tell your child that God trains us because he loves us. He wants us to keep going on our journey to know and love him so that someday we can be together forever.

### FAMILY Fun

Add in "milestones" to your training to keep each other motivated. At regular intervals, celebrate how far you've come and enjoy a treat or special reward together.

## CHAT **Prompts**

What has been the hardest part of our training? What motivates you to keep going?

# ELEMENTARY **Kids**

With your child, choose something you can train for together, and make a plan with a starting point and a finish line. Create a chart or mark off training times on a calendar, and encourage each other as you go. If your child wants to quit, encourage them, but let them know that it's your job to keep them on track so they finish their training. When you reach your finish line, celebrate together! Then read Proverbs 3:12, explaining that God trains us to reach the finish line of eternity with him.

# CHAPTER 50

# God Will Be Your Father

 **MEDITATE**

*The Spirit you received does not make you slaves, so that you live in fear again; rather, the Spirit you received brought about your adoption to sonship. And by him we cry, "Abba, Father." The Spirit himself testifies with our spirit that we are God's children.* – Romans 8:15-16

Extended passage: Romans 8:14-17

 **ANTICIPATE**

● What family story do your children love to hear?

_____

_____

● What do you remember most about your father?

_____

_____

I love to tell my kids stories about my family. Perhaps one of the most miraculous family stories I have is about my dad. When my dad was only two months old, his father died. And this loss, which you might be feeling acutely due to growing up without a father or because your children are growing up today without a father, twisted my dad. He grew up angry.

## TROUBLEMAKER

My dad was angry at his mother. He was angry at his father. He was angry at God for having left him without a father. He wondered, "God, how could you do this? And so my dad was a troublemaker, a rabble rouser, a ruffian during his elementary years. And as he grew older, he moved as far from God as he possibly could. Everything you can imagine in his teen and early adult life – until his Heavenly Father came to get him. The story of his conversion is as gripping as it miraculous.

## A PRAYER

Months after my dad trusted Christ, an elderly woman came up to him at the end of the service. This woman remembered my dad as a baby and she attended his father's funeral. During that funeral, she committed herself to pray for my dad every day so he would come to know God as his Heavenly Father. Take a minute to think about that – a child, lost without a dad, was prayed for daily by an elderly woman for nearly 25 years. And at the end of her life, she was able to hear that prayer answered.

## THIS UNSHAKEABLE PROMISE

Don't miss the importance of this promise: God will be your Father. And this is not based on anything you do or say. In fact, God chose you before you could do anything to convince him otherwise. He chose you intentionally and purposefully. Your identity is wrapped up in this promise of God, and as such it is firm and unshakeable, it is rooted in God's eternal purposes and glorious grace. Rest in this foundational promise of your Heavenly Father.

**AT HOME** The verse you read this week presents a stark contrast. You are not a slave to fear. You are a child of God. No matter what anyone says or how you feel, regardless of the relationship you have with your earthly father or your children have with their earthly father, this truth remains. Your Heavenly Father, through his Spirit, is bringing about your adoption. This week, rest in this deep truth. Embrace it. Remind yourself and your family of it.

## PRESCHOOL Kids

Create a safe place for a discussion with your preschooler and ask, "Is there anything that scares you? Tell me about that. Are you scared of those things when I am with you? Does being around me help those scary feelings go away?" Explain, "The Bible tells us the things we get scared of do not need to keep us full of scared feelings because God is our Heavenly Father. And Father is a name we can call God." When you pray, help your child refer to God as "Father."

### FAMILY Fun

Pick a night and tell stories about parents and grandparents. What do you remember? What did you enjoy doing together? What did you love most?

## CHAT Prompts

Throughout the Scripture, references to God as Father are numerous. One of the most famous references is in Jesus's prayer beginning with the words, "Our Father who art in heaven…" As a family, discuss where you think God is. Where does he live?

## ELEMENTARY Kids

Make a family tree. Kids really enjoy finding out how their family extends beyond the people they know and see with regularity. Read the passage together and look at the family tree you created. Ask them, "What does everyone in this family tree have in common?" Help them discover similarities. Read Romans 8:15-16 together and remind your child that all of the people you listed are children of God and he is their Heavenly Father.

# CHAPTER 51

# God Will Deliver Justice

*God's chosen people cry out to him day and night. Won't he make things right for them? Will he keep putting them off? I tell you, God will see that things are made right for them. He will make sure it happens quickly.* – Luke 18:7-8a (NIRV)

Extended passage: Luke 18:1-8

● What do you see in the world that you feel compelled to change?

_____

_____

● What do you need God to "make right" in your life?

_____

_____

I didn't set out to be a foster parent. In fact, like Jonah hunkered down on a boat headed in the opposite direction of Ninevah, I avoided it, choosing instead to work with at-risk children in other ways. And yet God pursued me, so I found myself standing in a courtroom on a handful of occasions, advocating for the best interest of a little girl who called me Mama for almost two years. I know what it's like to pray desperately for justice, and to stand in front of an unjust judge. I've seen what happens when a child falls through the cracks of our legal system and I've felt the frustration of waiting for God to make things right. This very verse was hope I clung to when all else failed. And while justice didn't come in the time or the way I expected, looking back I can see how all along God was making things right for a little girl who learned to call him Father.

## GOD IS JUST

This parable paints the contrast of a flawed human who offers justice out of annoyance with a God who makes things right for his children, whom he loves. Jesus told this story to encourage his followers to pray and not give up. To hold onto hope, though all else fails. What I learned from a courtroom echoes in this story: God is just and while I don't always understand his plan, I can trust in his promise.

## TRUSTING GOD'S PROMISE

Our children learn early that Life's Not Fair. They see injustice in classrooms and playgrounds, on television and movie screens, and as image bearers of God they will always long for a world where things are made right. We can teach them that God will make all things right but the tension is in the timing. Jesus's parable promises that God will bring justice quickly, and while we know God's promises are true, we don't always see the intricate details of God's handiwork unfolding. We have to choose to root our faith in God's promises even when we don't understand God's plan. And as we wait, we can cry out night and day, knowing that God hears us and is working to set things right.

# ON THE ROAD

**BEFORE BED** Fear is something we all face, and our children need to know that they can cry out to God, day or night. Remind your child of this before they go to bed, when fear of the dark and recurring nightmares often cause anxiety. Teach them to call out to God and trust that he will answer.

## PRESCHOOL Kids

No doubt you've been summoned to your preschooler's room many a time to calm their fears. Nightmares, monsters under the bed, or simply the anxiety of being alone can often cause sleep regression in young children. Read Luke 18:7-8a to your child. Let them know that God is always with them, there to comfort and protect them, and will always hear them when they pray. When you put your preschooler to bed, pray with them. If they wake up afraid, pray with them. Encourage them to talk to God first, before they even call out for you. Pray that calling out to God for help will become a habit that they will continue throughout their lives.

### FAMILY Fun

Play a game of catch. Blindfold your child and spin them a few times. Tell them they can call out to you and you will answer. Move slowly around the room. Say, "I'm here" when they call out. Remind them that God always answers when we call.

## CHAT **Prompts**

What are some worries or problems you are facing? How do you need God to help you?

# ELEMENTARY **Kids**

Older children have outgrown many of their imaginary fears but are more aware of and struggle with injustice in the world around them. They worry about bullying, divorce, death, serious illness, often because they are aware of these things happening in the lives of their friends and family. Take time before your child goes to bed each night to ask them what concerns they have. Then pray with them and for them, and for people they are concerned about. Read the story of the unjust judge in Luke 18, and ask your child what they think it means. Reassure them that they can call out to God day or night, and that he is always at work in their life and in the world, even if we don't understand his plan or timing.

## CHAPTER 52

# God Will Listen

 **MEDITATE**

*Before they call I will answer; while they are still speaking I will hear.*
*– Isaiah 65:24*

Extended passage: Isaiah 65:17-25

 **ANTICIPATE**

● When was a time you cried out to God?

_____

_____


● What is your response when your child cries out to you?

_____

_____

Our family recently got hit with a brutal round of the stomach flu. Kids were sleeping with buckets, in hallways outside of the bathroom, and on layers of waterproof bedding. We don't mess around with The Bug. For several nights, no matter how deep of a sleep I was in, I'd bolt at the sound of a cough down the hall. One night I heard my three-year-old Zion whimper, and I was at his side before he could even call for me. My Ninja skills are impressive when my kids are sick, which is ironic since most days I can't cross a room without tripping over the furniture.

## ANSWERING THE CALL

As a parent, when my child calls I answer without thinking. It's an automatic, instinctive response. In Isaiah we read that God will also answer when we call. But I love how he describes the "when" – "*before* they call I will answer." I set up baby monitors and leave doors cracked open because I want to be sure I hear my child's call. But God hears us even before we call, and not only does he promise to hear us, he promises to answer.

## A LOVING FATHER

This verse falls within a passage that describes the new heaven and the new earth. It speaks to the intimacy that will characterize that era, where God fully restores the relationship that was broken during the Fall. While God has not fully restored all things yet, it doesn't negate the fact that he desires to have an intimate relationship with us – he wants his children to call out when they need him, and we see that desire woven throughout Scripture. This promise is one of so many like it, that give us hope in a God who hears us and who is quick to answer when we call. As we travel along our faith journey, we don't know what's around the next bend. There will be difficult paths to traverse, but God sees them and he promises to answer before we even call out to him.

# ON THE ROAD

**BEDTIME** Your child has probably learned from experience that you will answer when they call for you. By answering their call, you are teaching them to trust you. Help them see that they can also trust God to answer their call.

## PRESCHOOL Kids

When you tuck your child in to bed tonight, tell them you're going to practice answering their call. If necessary, review the reasons they would need to call for you (when they're sick, if there's a fire, etc.). Tell them to wait until you've left, then call out for you. Respond immediately by returning to their side. Encourage your child to try calling loudly, then softly, while you stand outside their door and while you wait in another part of the house. Point out when you could hear their call, and when you couldn't. Share Isaiah 65:24 with your child, and let them know that God can always hear us even before we call.

## FAMILY Fun

Divide family members into two different rooms and try as many ways to talk. Call each other using cell phones, a baby monitor, two cups connected by string, or using animal calls. Which method was the most helpful? Which was the most fun? Which was loudest or hardest to hear?

## CHAT **Prompts**

If God hears us and promises to answer us even before we call, why do you think it's important to talk to God? What is the purpose of praying, or talking to God?

## ELEMENTARY **Kids**

Before putting your child to bed, tell them you're going to play a game. Have them hide somewhere in the house and call for you until you find them. Switch places – you hide and call for your child while they look for you. Do this a few times, then sit down together and read Isaiah 65:24. Ask your child when God promises to answer us. How can he answer even before we call? Share how this verse gives you comfort and hope, and pray together, thanking God that he promises to answer us even before we call.

# R❀SEKiDZ® New for Parents

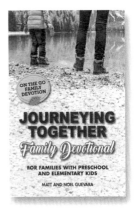

### New! On the Go Family Devotions: Journeying Together
#### A Devotional for Families with Children Ages 3-10
**Ages 3–10, 224 pages, 5½"x 8½" Paperback, Full Color Illustrations, Retail $16.99**

On The Go Family Devotions: Journeying Together takes the framework introduced in Deuteronomy 6 and applies to the daily life in the modern family. Each devotional gives parents ways to share their faith at home, on the road, when they wake up, and before they go to sleep. Each week, parents will engage in a devotion that centers them in Scripture and creates habits of engaging in casual conversations about God that will propel their child forward in their spiritual journey.

| On the Go: Journeying Together | L50006 | 9781628625011 | $16.99 |

## New! The Children's Rhyming Bible
### When a story rhymes, kids want to hear it all the time!
**Ages 3–7, 72 pages, 8"x 7" Hardcover, Full Color Illustrations, Retail $14.99**

Capture and keep your kids' attention with this beloved Children's Rhyming Bible. Featuring joyful illustrations, vivid colors, and a bouncing beat, this beloved Rhyming Bible tells 34 popular Bible stories in an engaging and unforgettable way.

From Creation and Noah's Ark to Jesus' Birth and Resurrection, boys and girls will love the delightful rhymes that will stick in their minds and help them hide God's Word in their hearts. Each Bible story is short, easy-to-read, and stays accurate to the Bible. Perfect for reading aloud to younger children, bedtime stories, or even for older children wanting to read the Bible to themselves.

| The Children's Rhyming Bible | L50004 | 9781628624991 | $14.99 |

# BEST-SELLING DEVOTIONALS FOR GIRLS!

## New! God and Me! for Little Ones
### My First Devotional for Toddler Girls Ages 2-3
**Ages 2–3, 32 pages, 8"x 8" Hardcover, Full Color Illustrations, Retail $9.99,**

This is the perfect first devotional for little girls ages 2-3. This Read-It-To-Me book helps toddler girls learn about God's love and care. Parents, grandparents and teachers can read the stories aloud to the child. Includes seven stories, each with Bible verse, question, and a prayer. Topics: Helping others, being thankful, trusting God, learning to obey, sharing, and being brave.

| My First Devotional for Toddler Girls | L46841 | 978-1-584111-82-5 | $9.99 |

## New! God and Me!
### A Devotional for Girls Ages 4-7
**Ages 4–7, 32 pages, 8"x  8" Hardcover, Full Color Illustrations, Retail $9.99,**

This new devotional for girls ages 4-7 helps them learn about God's love and care. Parents, grandparents and teachers can read the stories aloud to younger children. It includes seven stories, each with Bible verse, question, and a prayer. Topics: Knowing God, being thankful, trusting God, being kind, and God made me special.

| A Devotional for Girls Ages 4-7 | L46837 | 978-1-584111-73-3 | $9.99 |

# R☺SEKiDZ® New for Parents

## New! God and Me! 52 Week Devotional for Girls

**384–386 pages, 6"x 9" Softcover, Full Color Illustrations, Retail $14.99**

This devotional made for girls ages 6–9 and 10-12 covers situations you deal with at school and at home. Enjoy fully illustrated devotions as you are encouraged to rely on God by learning more about Him, His Word, and His plans for your life. Our unique 52-week devotional contains devotions and prayers on Days 1 through 5, and fun activities at the end of the week to reinforce the week's key Scripture memory verse and theme. Each day is designed to help you draw close to God.

| Ages 6-9 | L46838 | 978-1-584111-77-1 | $14.99 |
| Ages 10-12 | L46839 | 978-1-584111-78-8 | $14.99 |

## New! 52 Weekly Devotions for Busy Families

Enjoy having 52 weekly family devotions that you can do in as little as 5 minutes!

**Ages 4–12, 224 pages, 5½"x 7½" Paperback, Full Color Illustrations, Retail $16.99**

You want your children to get to know God better, but how do you do that? Between homework, errands, and extracurricular activities, it's hard to find time to get the whole family together. With such a packed schedule, how can you make room for devotions?

As short as 5 minutes or as long as an hour, the flexible design of this family devotional fits quality time and Bible learning right into your schedule! 52 Weekly Devotions for Busy Families gives you a plan to nurture your children's journey of faith with 5-minute devotionals and optional questions and activities to use throughout the week. If you're busy, just pick one idea. If you have more time, pick several of them! Perfect for families on the go!

| 52 Weekly Devotions for Busy Families | L50001 | 9781628625080 | $16.99 |

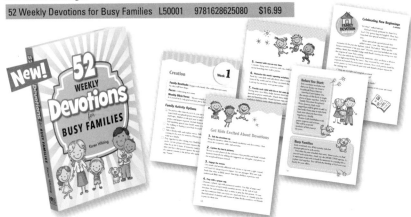